Restore the Hope
Devotions for Lent and Easter

By
Nancy J. Baker and Denise K. Loock

I pray God
will give you HOPE!
abundant
Nancy J. Baker

digdeeper
devotions

RESTORE THE HOPE: DEVOTIONS FOR LENT AND EASTER
BY NANCY J. BAKER AND DENISE K. LOOCK

Published by Dig Deeper Devotions
ISBN: 9781793060860
Copyright 2019 by Nancy J. Baker and Denise K. Loock
Cover and interior design by Lightning Editing Services

Available in print and as an ebook from amazon.com.

For more information on this book and the authors, visit digdeeperdevotions.com.

Printed in the United States of America

May our Lord Jesus Christ himself and God our Father, who loved us and by his grace gave us eternal encouragement and good hope, encourage your hearts and strengthen you in every good deed and work.

2 Thessalonians 2:16–17

Table of Contents

iii

iv

Beauty for Ashes

Many Christians see the value of observing a time of preparation for Easter. The solemn forty-day period known as Lent begins with Ash Wednesday and ends the Saturday before Easter. The forty days don't include Sundays, because Jesus rose from the dead on a Sunday.

The word *lent* comes from a Latin word meaning "spring."[1] Just as the winter months are a time of preparation for spring flowers, the Lenten season can help us prepare our hearts for the joyous celebration of Easter.

In biblical times, ashes symbolized grief, repentance, and feelings of unworthiness.[2] Some Christians still associate ashes with sorrow for sin and humble gratitude for God's forgiveness.

We can gain a fresh perspective on Easter by reviewing the Old Testament prophecies about the coming Messiah. Our excitement for Easter builds by reading the historical accounts of Matthew, Mark, Luke, and John as if we don't know what happens at the end of these books. We can imagine what Jesus's disciples and the other people he encountered thought of what he did and what he told them.

For example, one Sabbath day early in his ministry, Jesus entered the synagogue in his hometown, Nazareth. He stood to indicate that he wanted to speak that day and the leaders handed him the scroll. Unrolling it, he read from the book of Isaiah, chapter 61.

To provide hope for the Israelites, Isaiah prophesied that one day someone would be specially anointed by God to minister to the poor and brokenhearted, to mourners and prisoners—all who despaired. Instead of ashes on their heads, they'd receive crowns of beauty. They'd be anointed

1

with the oil of gladness and given garments of praise. They'd be called oaks of righteousness, planted by the Lord to display his splendor. Jesus ended his short sermon with an earthshaking statement: "Today this scripture is fulfilled in your hearing" (Luke 4:21 quoting Isaiah 61:1).

When Jesus finished speaking, the people of Nazareth murmured, "We know this man. This is Joseph's son," implying that Jesus couldn't be the One promised by Isaiah. Yet the gospels proclaim that Jesus fulfilled the prophet's words. Jesus came to the poor, the outcasts, and the diseased—all the people shunned by the religious leaders. He healed, he consoled, and he offered hope. He rebuilt ruined lives.

True, some of what he promised has not yet been fulfilled. People still mourn; they still despair. Others experience poverty or imprisonment. But the glimpses of Jesus's power and love revealed when he walked on earth give us hope—unwavering confidence that the rest of his promises will be fulfilled too, and much more.

As you prepare for Easter, dig deeper into what the Bible says about who Jesus is and why he came to earth. He is the only one who can transform ashes into beauty, despair into hope.

Part One

Old Testament Promises and Prophecies

Jesus said to the disciples, *"This is what I told you while I was still with you: Everything must be fulfilled that is written about me in the Law of Moses, the Prophets and the Psalms."*
Luke 24:44

Day 1
True Repentance[3]

I know that my redeemer lives, and that in the end he will stand on the earth. And after my skin has been destroyed, yet in my flesh I will see God; I myself will see him with my own eyes—I, and not another. How my heart yearns within me! Job 19:25–27

On Ash Wednesday, many Christians around the world put ashes on their forehead. This practice goes back to Old Testament times when putting ashes on one's head showed mourning or repentance. For example, when the Lord revealed his mighty power, Job replied, "My ears had heard of you, but now my eyes have seen you. Therefore I despise myself and repent in dust and ashes" (Job 42:5–6).

What is true repentance? To repent means "to change or turn another way." We may say, "I'm sorry." But the real issue is whether or not we have changed. Have we turned away from our sin?

One of the thieves crucified beside Jesus showed true repentance. Both thieves had been mocking Jesus (Matthew 27:44). But one paid attention when Jesus asked God to forgive those who mocked and crucified him. Awed that someone could do this, the thief's faith was kindled. He stopped mocking and said, "Jesus, remember me when you come into your kingdom" (Luke 23:42).

"Today you will be with me in paradise," Jesus assured him (Luke 23:43). Although the thief was helpless to show repentance by doing something, Jesus saw the man's faith and his changed heart.

5

I used to hurry over the somberness of Lent (especially Ash Wednesday) to the joyfulness of Easter. Now I meditate on my need for repentance—true repentance. I cannot live without sinning. I cannot do anything good enough to take away my own sins.

Jesus Christ, the sinless Son of God, bore all your sins himself on the cross. During this Lenten season, meditate on your need for repentance and accept the forgiveness Christ offers.

Reflections

_____

_____

_____

_____

_____

Dig Deeper

1. Read 2 Corinthians 7:8–11. What's the difference between "godly sorrow" and "worldly sorrow"?

2. Read Mark 2:15–17. What did Jesus tell the scribes and Pharisees when they asked why he associated with sinners? Why do you think the scribes and Pharisees didn't recognize that they were sinners too?

3. According to 1 John 1:9, what do we have to do to receive forgiveness for our sins both before and after we accept Christ as our Savior? What does 1 John 1:5–7 say about the evidence of true repentance in our lives?

Restore the Hope: Devotions for Lent and Easter

Day 2
The Light of the World

And God said, "Let there be light," and there was light. God saw that the light was good, and he separated the light from the darkness. Genesis 1:3–4

Our triune God transformed the universe by speaking light into existence on the first day of creation.[4] By dispelling the darkness, God created both a place for man to live and a means for him to live (days two and three). No light? No life. It's as simple as that.

The apostle John drew the connection between the creation of light in the physical world and the spiritual world when he declared that Jesus is the source of both kinds of light: "Through him all things were made . . . in him was life, and that life was the light of all mankind" (John 1:3–4). Paul also identified Jesus as the creator of all things, including light: "All things have been created through him and for him. He is before all things, and in him all things hold together" (Colossians 1:16–17).

When Jesus told the temple crowd he was the light of the world in John 8:12, he too connected the source of physical light with spiritual light. He said, "Whoever follows me will never walk in darkness, but will have the light of life." The Pharisees recognized the inference immediately and challenged him (v. 13). They knew God alone was the source of light and life. Jesus ended the debate by affirming his deity: "Before Abraham was, I AM." By using the name I AM, Jesus asserted his equality with Jehovah, the one true God who had revealed himself to Moses at the burning bush (v. 58, Exodus 3:13–14). But the enraged Pharisees

9

refused to accept that truth, so they picked up rocks to stone the "blasphemer."

Believing that Jesus is the Creator and the Sustainer of all things is fundamental to our faith. His authority over physical darkness symbolizes his authority over spiritual darkness. Each sunrise proclaims his dominion over physical darkness. On the cross, he permanently separated the darkness of sin from the light of righteousness. Each time the Holy Spirit empowers us to choose rightly, we affirm Jesus's dominion over spiritual darkness.

We can avoid all kinds of spiritual darkness—ignorance, error, doubt, confusion—because Jesus is the source of all light. Walking in light transforms us, providing the means for us to live prosperous, productive lives. No light? No life. It's as simple as that.

Live in the light.

Reflections

_____

_____

_____

_____

_____

Dig Deeper

1. Read Genesis 1. What other glimpses of Jesus can you see in the days of creation? What other parallels can you draw between the physical realm and the spiritual realm?

2. Read 2 Corinthians 4:3–6. What connection is Paul drawing between physical light and spiritual light? What prevents people from benefiting from spiritual light?

3. Read Matthew 5:14–16. Jesus also said that we, his followers, are the light of the world. How can the light we shed enable others to avoid spiritual darkness?

Day 3
The Victor over Sin and Death

God said, *"And I will put enmity between you and the woman, and between your offspring [seed] and hers; he will crush your head, and you will strike his heel."* Genesis 3:15

The Easter story is first presented in the Bible as a promise in the middle of a curse. When Adam and Eve sinned in the garden of Eden, God cursed the Serpent who had deceived and enticed them. "You will crawl on your belly and you will eat dust all the days of your life," he said (Genesis 3:14).

While we're glad to see the Serpent crawling and eating dust, we're not glad to see the enmity—war—between the Serpent and us. Yes, us. The war begun that day will continue until the end of time (Revelation 12:17).

In Genesis, God says the war will be waged between the two offspring. Beginning with Cain's murder of his brother, Abel, Satan has tried to destroy Adam and Eve's godly descendants; however, God preserved the line from Eve to Mary's son, Jesus (Luke 3:23–38).

When Jesus Christ was crucified, Satan thought he had won the war. But as Jesus had predicted, "Very truly I tell you, unless a kernel of wheat falls to the ground and dies, it remains only a single seed. But if it dies, it produces many seeds" (John 12:24). John sees the godly seed of Eve in a vision at the end of time, and they are too numerous to count (Revelation 7:9–10).

13

Jesus Christ not only arose from the dead, but his sacrifice for our sins also broke the power of death (Hebrews 2:14). He now sits at God's right hand, ruling over his enemies until they become a footstool beneath his scarred feet (Psalm 110:1–2).

On Easter, we celebrate Christ's victory over sin at the cross. We also celebrate a future triumph—the day when there will be no more sin and death: The Serpent will be thrown into the lake of fire to be tormented forever (Revelation 20:10). We'll eat the fruit of the tree of life (Revelation 22:3). There will be no more curse.

Are you joyfully anticipating that glorious day described by Paul when "the God of peace will soon crush Satan under your feet" (Romans 16:20)?

Reflections

_____

_____

_____

_____

_____

14

Dig Deeper

1. Read Genesis 3:17–20 and 4:1. Based on Adam's words and actions after he received the news about the curse of toiling, sweating, and returning to the dust from which he came, how do we know he still had hope? What does Eve's name mean?

2. Read 1 John 3:7–12. Is it possible to know the difference between the two sides in the war? How are the ones born of God distinguished from the children of the devil? Which of these characteristics do you see in your life?

3. You may know about the new heaven and new earth described in Revelation 21, but what's going to happen to the earth and to us according to Romans 8:18–23? Are you expecting? Groaning?

Day 4
A Pleasing Sacrifice

The Lord looked with favor on Abel and his offering.
Genesis 4:4

One word characterized Abel's life—*favor*. Other Bible translations use *respect*, *regard*, or *accept*. All the words indicate that Abel and his sacrifice pleased God.

For centuries, scholars have debated what made Abel's sacrifice acceptable and Cain's unacceptable. The primary issue, however, is what made Abel's life acceptable.

In Matthew 23:35, Jesus described Abel as "righteous." Hebrews 11:4 explains why Abel stood in a blameless position before God: "By faith Abel offered to God a more acceptable sacrifice" (ESV). Abel's heart condition—his faith—pleased God. He always looks at the contents of our hearts before he looks at an offering in our hands.

In obedience, Abel also offered a blood sacrifice, a precedent God established when he provided animal skins for Adam and Eve after they sinned (Genesis 3:21). God never changes. Scripture affirms, "Without the shedding of blood there is no forgiveness" (Hebrews 9:22; Leviticus 17:11). In faith, Abel was mindful of what pleased God and honored it.

Both Abel's heart and his sacrifice foreshadow Jesus Christ. First, Jesus stood in a blameless position before God because he was sinless. At Jesus's baptism, God the Father said, "This is my Son . . . with him I am well pleased" (Matthew 3:17). Jesus alone could say, "I always do what pleases [God]" (John 8:29).

17

Second, Jesus's battered, bleeding body was the sacrifice that permanently satisfied God's standard of righteousness. By faith, we stand righteous before God because Jesus offered the perfect sacrifice on our behalf (Hebrews 10:10). What sacrifice does God want us to bring? Consider the words of Elisha Hoffman's classic hymn, "Is Your All on the Altar?"

> Would you walk with the Lord,
> In the light of his Word,
> And have peace and contentment alway?
> You must do his sweet will, to be free from all ill,
> On the altar your all you must lay.
>
> Is your all on the altar of sacrifice laid?
> Your heart does the Spirit control?
> You can only be blest,
> And have peace and sweet rest,
> As you yield him your body and soul.*

Because of Jesus's death and resurrection, God's favor is forever available to those who, like Abel, offer the right sacrifice with the right heart. Does God look with favor on you?

*Complete lyrics of hymns mentioned in the book follow the devotion in which they are mentioned.

Reflections

_____

_____

_____

_____

_____

Dig Deeper

1. Read Hebrews 11:4 and Hebrews 12:24. What other connections do you see between Abel's life and Jesus's life? Why does the blood of Jesus speak "a better word" than the blood of Abel? (Compare Matthew 23:35–36 with 1 John 1:7.)

2. Read Genesis 4:1–7. How did God respond to Cain's unacceptable offering? How does he respond to us when we do wrong? What should Cain have done after God spoke to him? What should be our response to reproof?

3. Read Psalm 51:15–17 and Micah 6:6–8. What do these passages say about the kind of sacrifices that please God?

"Is Your All on the Altar?"
Elisha Hoffman, 1900, public domain

You have longed for sweet peace,
And for faith to increase,
And have earnestly, fervently prayed;
But you cannot have rest,
Or be perfectly blest,
Until all on the altar is laid.

Refrain:
Is your all on the altar of sacrifice laid?
Your heart does the Spirit control?
You can only be blest,
And have peace and sweet rest,
As you yield Him your body and soul.

Would you walk with the Lord,
In the light of His word,
And have peace and contentment alway?
You must do His sweet will,
To be free from all ill,
On the altar your all you must lay.

Oh, we never can know
What the Lord will bestow
Of the blessings for which we have prayed,
Till our body and soul
He doth fully control,
And our all on the altar is laid.

Who can tell all the love, He will send from above,
And how happy our hearts will be made;
Of the fellowship sweet
We shall share at His feet,
When our all on the altar is laid.

21

Day 5
Our High Priest Forever

The Lord has sworn and will not change his mind: "You are a priest forever, in the order of Melchizedek." Psalm 110:4

Some people go to a priest because they have sinned. They confess their sin to him, and he suggests an act of contrition (punishment) and offers absolution (forgiveness for the sin). Unfortunately, they will sin again and have to repeat the whole process.

In the Old Testament, God gave a similar system to Israel. When the people sinned, they went to a priest. He offered a sacrifice—an animal that died in their place—and they received forgiveness. When they sinned again, they returned to the priest. Once a year, the high priest offered a sacrifice that covered the sins of all the Israelites. But he too repeated the ritual every year. Sin was still a problem.

Long before Israel's sacrificial system existed, Abraham met Melchizedek, an unusual priest. Although most people worshiped many gods at this time, he worshiped only one: the Most High God, as did Abraham (Genesis 14:17–24). Melchizedek offered bread and wine to Abraham; Abraham then honored Melchizedek by giving him a tithe of the goods he'd recovered in a recent battle.

The meaning of their brief encounter is explained in other Scriptures. For example, the writer of the book of Hebrews notes this about Melchizedek: "Without father or mother, without genealogy, without beginning of days or end of life, resembling the Son of God, he remains a priest

23

forever" (7:3). Under the Mosaic law, priests had been appointed by ancestry—they all descended from Aaron. In contrast, Melchizedek, like Jesus Christ, was appointed by God. Therefore, both hold their priestly position forever.

Melchizedek's name means "my king is righteousness."[5] Of course he wasn't perfectly righteous; he was human and sinned like everyone else. Jesus Christ, however, is perfectly righteous: "one who is holy, blameless, pure, set apart from sinners, exalted above the heavens" (Hebrews 7:26).

When we sin, we come to Jesus, our perfect High Priest, because his sinless life and sacrificial death forever satisfied the standard of righteousness God established. Through his death on the cross, Jesus removed our sins and gave us his righteousness. We are forever forgiven.

Have you brought your sins to Jesus Christ? Do you live in the freedom of his forgiveness?

Reflections

Dig Deeper

1. In Genesis 14:17–24, read about Abraham's encounter with Melchizedek, who was not only a priest of the Most High God but also the king of Salem (possibly a shortened version of the word *Jerusalem*). What does Abraham do when he meets this man?

2. Read Hebrews 7:1–28. How does Jesus Christ meet the qualifications needed for a high priest in the order of Melchizedek?

3. Who is described in Revelation 5:6–14 as "a kingdom and priests to our God," and where will they reign? Picture yourself among the people described and praise God with the words they used in verses 12 and 13.

Day 6
The Power of Intercession

Then Abraham approached [God] and said, "Will you sweep away the righteous with the wicked? What if there are fifty righteous people in [Sodom and Gomorrah]?"
Genesis 18:23–24

When Abraham looked across the valley and saw the smoke rising from Sodom and Gomorrah, did he think his intercessory prayers for their inhabitants had failed? When he learned that only Lot and his daughters had survived, did he wonder if any good could ever come from such tragedy?

Abraham's intercession foreshadows Jesus's role as our divine intercessor. Before Jesus rode the donkey through the streets of Jerusalem, he stopped at the crest of the hill that overlooked the city and wept. "If you, even you, had only known on this day what would bring you peace—but now it is hidden from your eyes" (Luke 19:42). And earlier in the week he had cried, "Jerusalem, Jerusalem . . . how often I have longed to gather your children together, as a hen gathers her chicks under her wings, and you were not willing" (Matthew 23:37).

Jesus saw both the physical and the spiritual destruction that loomed over Jerusalem's inhabitants. The Romans destroyed the city less than forty years later (in AD 70), demolishing the temple and slaughtering thousands. More perilous, however, was the people's spiritual condition. On Sunday, many people lined the streets and shouted, "Hosanna! Hosanna!" Four days later, some of them yelled, "Crucify Him! Crucify Him!"

27

Jesus also interceded for the disciples who abandoned him when he was arrested (John 17:6–19). On the cross, he prayed for his executioners: "Father, forgive them, for they do not know what they are doing" (Luke 23:34). Our risen Lord continually intercedes for us so he can present us to God the Father "without fault" (Jude 1:24).

God is ever able to bring beauty out of destruction. Out of the ashes of Sodom and Gomorrah, God fashioned the everlasting dynasty of David's kingdom through one of Lot's descendants. (Compare Genesis 19:37 with Ruth 1:4, 4:13–22.) Overcoming their failure in Gethsemane, the disciples fearlessly spread the gospel throughout the world. Out of the bloodstained beams of Calvary's cross, God fashioned redemption, giving each of us an inheritance in Jesus's everlasting kingdom.

Never despair when the smoke of judgment clouds the sky. Pray, as both Abraham and Jesus did. God's mercy is boundless; his creativity is unfathomable. We may never know this side of heaven what masterpiece he's making out of the fragments of our intercessory prayers. That truth inspires me to keep praying. How about you?

Reflections

_____

_____

_____

_____

_____

Dig Deeper

1. Read Genesis 18. What connection do you see between verses 1–19 and verses 20–33? What enabled Abraham to be an effective intercessor?

2. Read Exodus 32:11–14, 30–35. On what basis does Moses ask God to be merciful? In what way does Moses's request in verses 31–32 foreshadow Christ?

3. Read Luke 19:41–44. What did Jesus see as he looked at the city of Jerusalem? What do you see when you look at your city?

Day 7
The Forgiver

"So then, don't be afraid. I will provide for you and your children." And [Joseph] reassured them and spoke kindly to them. Genesis 50:21

No Old Testament character typifies Jesus Christ in more ways than Joseph. In fact, Arthur Pink draws over 100 parallels in his classic, *Gleanings in Genesis*: beloved by their fathers, hated by their brothers, falsely accused, considered criminals, exalted to a high position, and provided deliverance for their people, to name a few.[6] None of those connections, however, squeeze my heart like the one recorded in Genesis 50.

Joseph's brothers and his father, Jacob, had been living in Egypt for seventeen years when Jacob blessed his sons on his deathbed (Genesis 49). After the burial and mourning, the brothers feared Joseph would finally pay them back for selling him into slavery (Genesis 50:15).

They'd lived under the weight of their guilt for two decades in Canaan before famine forced them to go to Egypt. They continued to carry their guilt after Joseph revealed his identity, told them they were forgiven, and then demonstrated his love the rest of their lives.

Joseph could've forgiven them, sent them back to Canaan with sufficient supplies, and ignored them. But he didn't. He invited them to live in Egypt, provided them with a livelihood, and pursued a relationship with them. When his elder brothers came to him after Jacob's death, fearful that he'd exact the vengeance they assumed he always wanted,

Joseph wept. Why? He was overcome by their inability to live like they were forgiven. He had forgotten; why couldn't they?

How often do we act like Joseph's brothers? We live in fear that somehow, in some way God will make us pay for past sins. We refuse to accept the forgiveness Jesus purchased for us at such great cost. How his heart must ache over such ignorant, ungrateful behavior. Jesus could've redeemed us, then sent us down life's road alone. But he refuses to do that. In love, he seeks an intimate relationship with us. And he pushes us toward our potential because he is determined to complete the good work he has begun in us (Philippians 1:6).

What wondrous love is this! Not only forgiven, but also befriended and beloved. May we live victoriously, in the forgiveness and friendship that Jesus's death and resurrection provided.

Reflections

_____

_____

_____

_____

_____

Dig Deeper

1. Read Genesis 50:15–26. More than fifty years elapsed between verses 21 and 24. Do you think the elder brothers had finally learned to accept Joseph's forgiveness? Why or why not?

2. Do you struggle to accept forgiveness as Joseph's brothers did? Meditate on these verses: Psalm 103:8–14, Lamentations 3:22–26, Hebrews 10:15–23, 1 John 1:9.

3. Read 1 John 4:7–21. How can we love as Joseph and Jesus loved?

Day 8
The Anointed One, Son, and King

I will proclaim the Lord's decree: He said to me, "You are my son; today I have become your father." Psalm 2:7

How can God be One in Three Persons? I don't claim to understand the Triune God, but as I study the Scriptures, I see three Persons—sometimes all three in one verse. In Psalm 2, I see the Father and the Son.

In this psalm, David connected God's Anointed One (v. 2), his King (v. 6), and his Son (vv. 7–12) with Zion, another name for Jerusalem (v. 6).[7] To be anointed was to be set apart, consecrated, holy unto the Lord. The Jews used anointing oil to consecrate priests (Exodus 30:30), kings (1 Samuel 10:1; 16:13), and prophets (Isaiah 61:1).

When Jesus called God his Father, some Jews were infuriated and wanted to stone him to death for blasphemy. But others remembered Scriptures such as Psalm 2, which prophesied that the coming Messiah would be called God's Son. "You are the Christ, the Son of the living God," Peter told Jesus (Matthew 16:16 NKJV). He used the Greek *Christos*, The Anointed One."[8] Martha said, "You are the Messiah, the Son of God, who is to come into the world" (John 11:27).

Jesus totally baffled most of the Jews, and we may be baffled too. How did God become his Father *today* (Psalm 2:7)? Jesus was not created; he created everything (Colossians 1:16–17). He has always existed as God (John 1:1, 14). But he entered time and became the begotten Son

35

of God. He took on flesh and became a baby—the Anointed Son, our Savior.

Psalm 2 is prophetic. Although the whole world—except for a remnant—will band together to conspire against God and his Anointed One, God will laugh (Psalm 2:1–4). He will continue to sit on his heavenly throne, sovereignly in control of everything. He has promised his Son the ends of the earth as his inheritance (v. 8). The Son will one day take a rod of iron to God's enemies, dashing them to pieces like pottery (v. 9).

But before judgment comes, there's a warning. "Kiss his Son," David wrote (v. 12). Some will receive the Son's anger and be destroyed, but some will be blessed and take refuge in him.

During this Lenten season and throughout the rest of your life, will you "kiss" Jesus—honor him and submit to him as God the Father's Anointed One, his Son, and the rightful king of all nations?

Reflections

_____

_____

_____

_____

_____

Dig Deeper

1. According to John 10:36–42, how did Jesus back up his claim to be the Son of God?

2. Read Hebrews 1:1–5. How did the writer of Hebrews describe the relationship between God and Jesus? What is Jesus doing (v. 4)? How does that impact your life?

3. As many in the world seem to be turning away from God, Colossians 3:1–4 is a good passage to memorize and to keep in mind. What is Jesus doing? Where are you in this picture?

Day 9
Suffering and Sacrifice

For [the Lord] has not despised or scorned the suffering of the afflicted one; he has not hidden his face from him but has listened to his cry for help. Psalm 22:24

When David wrote about his suffering in Psalm 22, did he know his words were prophetic? In the psalm, he graphically described in great detail something that would happen two thousand years later: the crucifixion of Jesus Christ. David felt forsaken when he cried out day and night to God but received no answer (Psalm 22:1–2). Similarly, after a night and day of cruel beatings and false accusations, Jesus was nailed to a cross. There, he cried out in a loud voice, "My God, my God, why have you forsaken me?" (Mark 15:34).

We sometimes feel like God has forsaken us when our sins separate us from him. But he will never forsake us (Hebrews 13:5). Because of Jesus's perfect, once-for-all sacrifice, we can confess our sins and receive forgiveness (Hebrews 9:24–26).

David wrote, "I am poured out like water, and all my bones are out of joint. My heart has turned to wax; it has melted within me. My mouth is dried up like a potsherd, and my tongue sticks to the roof of my mouth … they pierce my hands and my feet … people stare and gloat over me … They divide my clothes among them and cast lots for my garment" (Psalm 22:14–18). Was this David's experience, or did he see it in a vision as he wrote? (Compare Psalm 22 and Matthew 27:27–31.)

Is there any pain we experience that Jesus didn't experience? He was rejected by his own people and subjected to a cruel punishment. David prayed, "Deliver me from the sword, my precious life from the power of the dogs" (Psalm 22:20). How interesting that Jesus died before the Roman soldier pierced his side with a sword (John 19:30–35).

Three days after his horrible death, Jesus Christ rose victoriously from the grave. Psalm 22:30–31 says that people from all the ends of the earth will turn to the Lord, and "they will proclaim his righteousness, declaring to a people yet unborn: He has done it!" Two thousand years after the resurrection of Jesus Christ, people from all over the world have heard and believed.

Are you committed to serve the risen, righteous Perfect Sacrifice? Do you praise him for his victory over sin and proclaim, "He has done it"?

Reflections

_____

_____

_____

_____

_____

Dig Deeper

1. Read Exodus 12:43–46, Psalm 34:19–20, John 19:31–37, and 1 Peter 1:17–20. Why is it significant that none of Jesus's bones were broken?

2. According to Zechariah 12:10 and Revelation 1:5–7, what is the result of Jesus Christ's sacrifice? Have you been washed from your sins by his blood, or will you be among the wailers?

3. Using only the Bible verses cited in this devotion—including the questions—can you state what has been fulfilled that was written about Jesus Christ in the law, the prophets, and the psalms (Luke 24:44)?

Day 10
In God's Hands

But I trust in you, Lord; I say, "You are my God." My times are in your hands; deliver me from the hands of my enemies, from those who pursue me. Let your face shine on your servant; save me in your unfailing love. Psalm 31:14–16

David wrote, "My life is consumed by anguish and my years by groaning; my strength fails because of my affliction, and my bones grow weak. Because of all my enemies, I am the utter contempt of my neighbors and an object of dread to my closest friends—those who see me on the street flee from me" (Psalm 31:10–11). He even cried in alarm that he was cut off from God (31:22).

Anguish, groaning, affliction, and weakness, along with neighbors showing contempt, friends dreading his presence, and people fleeing from him—David easily could've been overwhelmed by such feelings and thoughts. Instead he turned to God: "My times are in your hands; deliver me ... shine your face on me ... save me." He trusted God's unfailing love.

As Jesus set his face toward Jerusalem a few days before Passover, he knew what lay before him. He was walking into the net his enemies were preparing for him. He would suffer many things at the hands of the elders, the chief priests, and the teachers of the law. They would condemn him to death and hand him over to the Gentiles to be mocked, flogged, and crucified (Matthew 16:21, 20:17–19).

43

Jesus knew his disciples would scatter just as David's friends had fled (Matthew 26:31, 56). When Jesus bore the sins of the world, he would experience the loneliness of God the Father turning his back on the sin (Matthew 27:46). Even so, Jesus would say as David did, "Into your hands I commit my spirit" (Psalm 31:5; Luke 23:46).

As Jesus faced crucifixion, he also trusted God's unfailing love. After three days in the tomb, Jesus rose from the dead (Matthew 20:19). He knew his death meant new life for us.

Do you know that when you say, "You are my God; my times are in your hands," that he extends his unfailing love to you? That love provides strength and comfort when you feel overwhelmed. You too will triumph over your enemies and rise again to everlasting life.

Are you feeling safe in God's hands today?

Reflections

_____

_____

_____

_____

_____

Dig Deeper

1. According to 2 Corinthians 4:16–18, what should be our perspective as we face troubles?

2. What promises are given in Psalm 31? Although his enemies did kill Jesus, how would these verses have comforted him? In what ways do these verses comfort you?

3. The truths of Psalm 23 must have encouraged David as they have encouraged many others. Read verses 4–6. The rod and staff were used to guide, defend, and sometimes to rescue sheep.[9] How has your Shepherd guided, defended, or rescued you? How has he comforted you?

Day 11
Transforming Trials into Triumph

Do not be far from me, O Lord. Awake, and rise to my defense! Contend for me, my God and Lord. Psalm 35:22–23

False accusations. Ruthless witnesses. Gloating adversaries. How can such a scenario end in triumph, not tragedy? Yet that's the progression of David's Psalm 35. In it, he described an unjust lawsuit, which foreshadowed Jesus's trials before the Sanhedrin and Pilate almost 1,000 years later.

In his psalm, David began with a plea for God to be both his defense lawyer and his avenging warrior (vv. 1–3). As unlikely as it appeared at the time, God was wielding his sword as he battled David's enemies. And centuries later, God was battling Satan's forces at Jesus's trials even when it seemed his enemies had won.

David asked God to defend him against those "who seek my life and ... plot my ruin" (Psalm 35:4). In Jesus's case, the religious leaders were the murderous plotters. Matthew wrote, "The chief priests and the whole Sanhedrin were looking for false evidence against Jesus so that they could put him to death. But they did not find any, though many false witnesses came forward" (26:59–60). Truly, they "dug a pit" for Jesus "without cause" (Psalm 35:7).

David also wrote, "Assailants gathered against me without my knowledge. They slandered me without ceasing. Like the ungodly, they maliciously mocked; they gnashed their teeth at me" (Psalm 35:15–16). Luke recorded, "The men

47

who were guarding Jesus began mocking and beating him. They blindfolded him and demanded, 'Prophesy! Who hit you?' And they said many other insulting things to him" (22:63–65).

David could've concluded that God had abandoned him, but he chose to praise and trust God despite his circumstances (Psalm 35:27–28). During Jesus's trial and crucifixion, it seemed like God the Father had abandoned his Son too. But Jesus knew the Father's temporary silence was working toward the glorious triumph over death, which would provide eternal salvation for all of us.

Seasons of adversity are challenging, but as surely as God brought David and Jesus through the trials and into triumph, he will do the same for us. Therefore, like David, we can remain hopeful and claim victory in advance. With him, we can say, "My tongue will speak of your righteousness and of your praises all day long" (Psalm 35:28).

What praise will you offer to God today?

Reflections

Dig Deeper

1. How do you respond when others attack you "without cause"? Meditate on Isaiah 35:3–4, 53:10–12, and 54:16–17. Then ask God to help you respond with grace.

2. Compare David's request in Psalm 35:4–6 with Revelation 21:8. What is the ultimate end of false witnesses and those who mock the godly? Are you willing to allow God to handle them?

3. In chapters 13–16 of his gospel, John records Jesus's actions and teachings during the Last Supper. Jesus quoted Psalm 35:19 in John 15:25. How do his words to the disciples in John 15:18–27 and John 16:33 encourage you?

Day 12
Which Jesus Are You Worshiping?

The Lord says to my Lord: Sit at my right hand until I make your enemies a footstool under your feet. Psalm 110:1

Psalm 110 declares emphatically that the resurrection power of Easter endures forever, and it should impact our lives every day. This psalm, written by David, is quoted or alluded to more than any other psalm in the New Testament.[10] Why is it so important?

Consider what Peter said on Pentecost. As he explained who Jesus truly was, Peter said, "God has raised this Jesus to life ... exalted to the right hand of God" (Acts 2:32–33). Then he quoted Psalm 110:1 and proclaimed, "God has made this Jesus, whom you crucified, both Lord and Messiah" (v. 36). He also exhorted the crowd to acknowledge Jesus as the Messiah, David's heir, and to repent of their sins. The power that raised Jesus from the dead could transform their lives (vv. 38–39). And it did (vv. 40–47).

Psalm 110:4–5 explains what the risen Christ was doing for those first-century Christians as well as what he is doing for us. He sits at God's right hand as our high priest (v. 4). There, he intercedes for us, helping us become the holy servants we are designed to be (Hebrews 7:25–26; 10:12–13).

No wonder Psalm 110 filled the New Testament writers with joy and hope. It portrays Jesus as he is now, our royal high priest who reigns in heaven. We don't worship a Jesus nailed to a cross. Neither do we worship a Jesus standing by an empty tomb. We worship the Jesus who sits at the right hand of God the Father with power and authority.

This Jesus provides the forgiveness, strength, and hope we need to live and to serve him. And one day, this Jesus will lead his troops into the final battle against the forces of evil, and he will judge the nations (Psalm 110:1–3, 5–7). This Jesus has promised, "To him who overcomes, I will give the right to sit with me on my throne, just as I overcame and sat down with my Father on his throne" (Revelation 3:21).

Are you worshiping this Jesus?

Reflections

_____

_____

_____

_____

_____

Dig Deeper

1. The week Jesus was crucified, he quoted Psalm 110:1 at the temple. Read the gospel accounts in Matthew 22:41–46, Mark 12:35–37, and Luke 20:39–44. What question did Jesus ask? How did the crowd and the religious leaders respond to Jesus's words?

2. In Peter's sermon at Pentecost, he explained the importance of Psalm 110. Read his words in Acts 2:22–36. Can you explain the importance of the psalm in your own words?

3. Read Zechariah 6:9–15. How does this passage about a human priest, Joshua, echo the truths about Jesus provided in Psalm 110?

Day 13
The Suffering Servant of God

See, my servant will act wisely; he will be raised and lifted up and highly exalted. Just as there were many who were appalled at him—his appearance was so disfigured beyond that of any human being and his form marred beyond human likeness—so he will sprinkle many nations, and kings will shut their mouths because of him. For what they were not told, they will see, and what they have not heard, they will understand. Isaiah 52:13–15

How would you define *passion*? Do you think of it as a negative or a positive word? *Passion* describes both good and bad emotions. These are the deepest, most intense feelings we can have, such as passionate love or passionate anger.

Christians call the week concluding with Easter—Passion Week. The suffering Jesus endured on the cross is called "The Passion of Christ" because of the magnitude of his agony.

The intense suffering Jesus endured on the cross is beyond our comprehension. I remember reading an article in which a doctor described what happened to a person during crucifixion. I couldn't sleep that night; I was so filled with vivid images of what my Savior had suffered. It's a brutal, excruciating way to die.

Jesus suffered not only physical cruelty; he also suffered mental torment. Jesus had never before known separation from the Father, but as Jesus bore the sins of the whole world, the Father turned his back on his Son. The most passionate rage you've ever seen is nothing compared to God's anger at sin. We hear Jesus's anguished cry of abandonment, "My God (not My Father as Jesus usually addressed him), My God why have you forsaken me?" (Matthew 27:46) God had turned his back; his holiness could not look on sin.

But the Passion of Christ also reminds us of the good meanings of the word *passion*. God's love was present as well as his wrath. Just before Jesus died, he said, "It is finished" (John 19:30). He then called out with a loud voice, "*Father*, into your hands I commit my spirit" (Luke 23:46, emphasis added). Once the sin penalty had been paid, the Father and Son's fellowship was restored.

We know God's wrath was satisfied because Jesus rose from the dead. He had paid the penalty for sin through his suffering and death. Only a sinless person could pay that price as a perfect sacrifice and live to tell about it (Romans 6:23).

Isaiah said, "After he has suffered, he will see the light of life and be satisfied; by his knowledge my righteous servant will justify many, and he will bear their iniquities" (53:11). Jesus suffered for our sake, to bear the iniquities of every person and to justify those who would believe.

Do you believe this?

Reflections

_____

_____

_____

_____

Dig Deeper

1. Read Isaiah 52:13–14. What two extremes describe the Suffering Servant of God?

2. Read John 3:16–21. Why did God send his Son to die? What do these verses say about those who do not choose to believe in Jesus?

3. What reason does Luke give for Jesus's death and resurrection in chapter 24:46–47?

Part Two

New Testament
The Coming of the Messiah

Jesus said, *"The Spirit of the Lord is on me, because he has anointed me to proclaim good news to the poor. He has sent me to proclaim freedom for the prisoners and recovery of sight for the blind, to set the oppressed free, to proclaim the year of the Lord's favor."*
Luke 4:18–19

Day 14
The Miracle Worker

What Jesus did here in Cana of Galilee was the first of the signs through which he revealed his glory; and his disciples believed in him. John 2:11

Have you ever wondered why Jesus chose to turn water into wine as his first miracle? Mary told her son about the wine running out. Did she expect him to do a miracle?

Jesus didn't do the miracle to please his mother. He didn't do it as a gift to the bride and groom. He did it as a sign to reveal he was the Messiah for whom Israel had been waiting.

Knowing more about Jewish customs in Jesus's time is key to understanding the significance of the miracle at Cana. A Jewish marriage had two parts: (1) the betrothal (2) the wedding. The betrothal involved a ceremony where the couple legally became husband and wife.

After that ceremony, the bride continued to live with her family for a time, usually a year. Then the bridegroom and his friends came to her home with great ceremony, and the bridegroom took his betrothed to his home or the home of his father for the wedding feast. She then became his bride (she was already his wife legally).

Throughout the Old Testament, Israel was referred to as a wife. God had chosen Israel to be a unique nation, which he would guide and bless abundantly. But the nation was adulterous; the Israelites worshiped other gods.

The prophet Jeremiah said the voices of the bride and bridegroom would end in the land of Israel; that is, there would be weddings, but this imagery of God married to Israel would end (Jeremiah 7:30–35; 16:9). Israel hadn't acknowledged God as their provider, so he would remove the grain and the wine he'd given them.

But God gives second chances. The New Testament picks up the theme of the bridegroom. Shortly after he baptized Jesus, John the Baptist said, "The bride belongs to the bridegroom. The friend who attends the bridegroom waits and listens for him and is full of joy when he hears the bridegroom's voice. That joy is mine, and it is now complete" (John 3:29). The symbolism of wine is evident at the wedding in Cana—not with Jesus as the bridegroom but with his provision of heaven-sent wine.

Like the nation of Israel, we too are often adulterous, worshiping other gods such as money or celebrities. We also forget to acknowledge God's provision. But aren't you glad that Jesus, our Bridegroom, died for our sins so we could become his bride?

Reflections

_____

_____

_____

_____

_____

Dig Deeper

1. John the Baptist called himself the "friend who attends the bridegroom," someone we would call the "best man" or "groom's attendant." Why does Jesus call himself the bridegroom in Luke 5:33–35?

2. In Revelation 19:6–9, for whom is the bride dressed? Who is named as the bridegroom? Are you invited to the wedding?

3. Toward the end of his ministry on earth, what additional symbolic significance did Jesus attach to wine? Read Matthew 26:26–28.

Day 15
The Deliverer

You, dear children, are from God and have overcome them, because the one who is in you is greater than the one who is in the world. 1 John 4:4

Have you ever felt trapped, imprisoned, isolated, or hopeless? If so, you'll sympathize with a man who lived in the region of the Gerasenes. For many years, he hadn't lived in a house or worn clothes. When the townspeople tried to bind him with chains, the demon who lived inside him broke the chains. He was forced to live among the tombs (Luke 8:26–27).

But one day Jesus came to this area. When Jesus saw the demon-possessed man, he commanded the impure spirit to come out. The man fell at Jesus's feet, and shouted, "What do you want with me, Jesus, Son of the Most High God? I beg you, don't torture me!" (v. 28).

The evil being who'd overpowered the man cowered before the power of the Deliverer, the Son of the Most High God. One of the signs of Jesus's messiahship was his power over demons. He drove them out with a word.

Jesus asked the demon his name and he replied, "Legion." An army of demons! They begged Jesus to let them go into some pigs that were feeding on the hillside (vv. 31–32).

"Go," Jesus said. The demons went into the pigs. They rushed down the steep bank into the lake and were drowned. "When those tending the pigs saw what had happened, they ran off to report this in the town and countryside, and the people went out to see what had happened" (vv. 34–35).

The townspeople found the man sitting at Jesus's feet, dressed and in his right mind. They were overcome with fear and asked Jesus to go away.

Jesus then climbed into the boat to leave (vv. 36–37). But the man he'd delivered begged Jesus to let him go too. Instead, Jesus sent him home to share his story with the people in his town. They were so bound up in making a living they couldn't respond to the miracle in faith.

We too can be bound by jobs, by pleasing others, or more serious addictions. We need to fall at Jesus's feet and ask the Deliverer to set us free, help us live according to his will, and give us hope.

Reflections

_____

_____

_____

_____

_____

Dig Deeper

1. Read Luke 8:36–39. How do you think the townspeople reacted to the man's testimony? Do you think he would have stopped testifying if they mocked him? Have you ever experienced deliverance from a dreadful situation? Have you shared your story with others to glorify God?

2. Contrast the different responses of the demoniac and townspeople with the Philippians' responses in Acts 16:16–24. Who had wrong responses, and who had right ones?

3. What does 2 Peter 2:19–21 say about Christians turning to things that put them into bondage? How can we find freedom according to Romans 7:15–8:2?

Day 16
The Lord of Fish and Fishermen

Simon answered, "Master, we've worked hard all night and haven't caught anything. But because you say so, I will let down the nets." Luke 5:5

When's the last time you were awake all night? Was it due to work, illness, or travel? Were you anticipating a good experience or dreading a bad one?

Simon Peter and his brother, Andrew, had been up all night fishing. But they hadn't caught any fish. Probably not the first time the nets of these professional fishermen had come up empty. Nevertheless, the long hours of futile labor must have rankled the men as they washed their nets.

Then Jesus stepped into their boat and said, "Put out into deep water, and let down the nets for a catch" (Luke 5:4).

Simon Peter's answer betrayed his doubt: "Master ... we haven't caught anything." In other words, "Lord, we're the professionals. We know when and where the fish are most likely to be caught. If we've come up empty ..."

Still, a spark of faith glowed in these words: "because you say so." Peter and Andrew had traveled with Jesus throughout Galilee. They'd heard his authoritative teaching. They'd seen him cast out a demon and heal the sick (Luke 4:31–44).

They hadn't committed to full-time discipleship, but the time spent with Jesus had filled them with wonder and hope (see Luke 4:15, 22, 36). So when Jesus told them to throw the nets into the water, they obeyed. And they caught such a large number of fish that their nets nearly broke and the boat almost sank (Luke 5:6–7).

Peter didn't miss the lesson. The Master controlled the uncontrollable—fish in the sea. If he could do that, he was worthy to be followed, worthy to be worshiped. Peter then fell at Jesus's feet and said, "Go away from me, Lord; I am a sinful man!" (v. 8). This humble response signified a profound change in the proud fisherman.

Jesus turned the all-nighter into a life-changing experience for Peter as well as Andrew, James, and John. They "pulled their boats up on shore, left everything and followed [Jesus]" (v. 11).

What's keeping you up at night? Give it to Jesus. Obey his directives even if you waver between doubt and faith. He can take that spark of faith, rekindle your hope, and transform your life.

Reflections

_____

_____

_____

_____

_____

Dig Deeper

1. Read Matthew 8:5–13. Compare the centurion's faith in the Matthew passage to Peter's faith in Luke 5:1–11. Why do you think Jesus praised the centurion so highly?

2. Read Luke 4:31–44. What was Jesus revealing about himself in these situations? How has he demonstrated those truths about himself in your life?

3. To waver between faith and doubt is human. Read Mark 9:14–29 and James 1:5–8. What will help us replace our doubt with hope?

Day 17
The Bread of Life

Jesus said, *"I am the bread of life. ... This is the bread that came down from heaven. Your ancestors ate manna and died, but whoever feeds on this bread will live forever."* John 6:48, 58

Miracles. Jesus had fed 5,000 men plus women and children with two loaves of barley bread and two fish. After this miracle, the crowd wanted to make him king. But he sent his disciples ahead across the Sea of Galilee to Capernaum on a boat, while he withdrew to the mountain to be alone.

When a storm arose on the sea, Jesus walked on the water to the disciples. As he stepped into the boat, "immediately the boat reached the [opposite] shore" (John 6:21).

The crowds came to Capernaum seeking Jesus. He told them that they'd come because they wanted more physical bread. Instead, he offered them the true bread that comes from heaven. This bread was different from the manna from heaven God had given to the Israelites in the wilderness, different from the bread Jesus had given them earlier that day (vv. 31–33). Those breads didn't satisfy; they didn't give eternal life.

"I am the bread of life," Jesus told them, but "still you do not believe" (vv. 35–36). "I am the living bread that came down from heaven. Whoever eats this bread will live forever. This bread is my flesh, which I will give for the life of the world" (v. 51).

The crowd thought they knew who this man was; they knew his parents (vv. 41–42). When Jesus said these things, they were unable to see past the literal meaning. His words were too weird. Was he talking about cannibalism? (v. 52).

Jesus, however, was speaking of spiritual truths. He would become living bread to them by sacrificing his life on the cross.

Many took offense and went away (v. 66). Jesus then asked his disciples if they wanted to go away as well. Simon Peter answered him, "Lord, to whom shall we go? You have the words of eternal life. We have come to believe and to know that you are the Holy One of God" (vv.68–69). Peter had seen the miracles and received Jesus's words.

Do you receive afresh each day the Living Bread from heaven that satisfies like nothing on earth can? Or are you settling for spiritual junk food?

Reflections

_____

_____

_____

_____

_____

Dig Deeper

1. Read John 6:41–71. Contrast the responses of the crowd, Peter, and Judas. They all heard the same words and saw the same miracle of multiplied bread. What made the difference?

2. Compare Isaiah 55:1–2 and John 6:26–27. Do you seek Jesus mostly for the physical things he can give you? How can you change that habit? What spiritual things do you need from him right now?

3. According to 2 Corinthians 5:1–9, how can we gain and maintain an eternal perspective?

Day 18
The Good Shepherd

This is how we know what love is: Jesus Christ laid down his life for us. And we ought to lay down our lives for our brothers and sisters. 1 John 3:16

Jesus said, "I am the good shepherd." He then defined a shepherd's role by explaining, "The good shepherd lays down his life for the sheep" (John 10:11). But did he have more in mind than his death on the cross?

The Greek word translated "lays" in John 10:11 carries a twofold meaning: to kneel in humility and to construct a foundation.[11] Jesus did both. He humbled himself to become the permanent, atoning sacrifice for our sins (Philippians 2:8). He also constructed the foundational principles of the laying-down life for us to build on (1 Corinthians 3:11).

The Good Shepherd modeled the laying-down life on earth. First, during three years of ministry, he equipped his disciples to desire that life. Jesus then experienced an excruciating death to restore our relationship with God. The apostle John received that equipping and witnessed Jesus's death. Along with the other apostles, he not only observed what the laying-down life truly meant but also learned to practice it.

John said we demonstrate the love Jesus modeled when we "lay down our lives" for others. I grapple with that commandment daily. I don't want to lay down my life for others. I want to enjoy the attentive, loving care of the

Good Shepherd, but I'm often reluctant to put the needs of others above my own.

The Greek word translated "good" in John 10:11 suggests beneficence (see Romans 15:2; Ephesians 4:29). In other words, good is defined as that which benefits another person. In a spiritual context, that good includes directing someone toward choices that reap eternal benefits. Jesus did that while he lived on earth; now he does it in heaven as he intercedes for us (Hebrews 7:25; Jude 1:24–25).

Our Good Shepherd has equipped us for the laying-down life by giving us the Holy Spirit. Through him, we've been given "everything we need for a godly life"—working toward what is eternally best for ourselves and others (2 Peter 1:3).

Are we willing to follow the Good Shepherd's example? Will we humble ourselves and build on the foundation he laid?

Dear Shepherd, instill in my heart the desire to follow your example and strengthen my resolve to lay down my life for others.

Reflections

_____

_____

_____

_____

_____

Dig Deeper

1. Read John 10:10–17, 24–29. According to these verses, what other actions and attitudes characterize the Good Shepherd? What is the relationship between the Good Shepherd and his sheep?

2. Learning to model the laying-down life was a process for the disciples too. Read Mark 10:35–37 and Luke 9:51–56. What should John and James have done in these two instances?

3. Read Philippians 2:1–8. How would the problems of verses 1–4 be solved if we had the mind-set of Jesus and modeled the laying-down life?

Day 19
The Way, Truth, and Life

Jesus answered, "I am the way and the truth and the life. No one comes to the Father except through me." John 14:6

The Passover dinner conversation took an unexpected turn. First, Jesus said that one of the disciples would betray him (John 13:18). Then Jesus said something that chilled the disciples' souls: "I will be with you only a little longer. ... Where I am going, you cannot come" (v. 33).

Peter was the first to ask, "Where are you going?" (13:36). Jesus discerned the disciples' dismay; therefore he assured them that, although they couldn't accompany him at that time, they knew the way to his destination. But Thomas disagreed: "Lord, we don't know where you're going, so how can we know the way?" (John 14:5). Jesus answered with these familiar words: "I am the way, the truth, and the life."

On the eve of his crucifixion, Jesus tried to prepare the disciples for what lay ahead, but they seemed fixated on the loss of his presence (see also John 16:16–18). Peter's question—"Where are you going?"—hung in the room like a dense fog, obscuring everything else Jesus said.

When unexpected or devastating events confound us, Jesus's words to his disciples that night can clear our vision. First, the balm for troubled souls is, as Jesus said, "Trust in God; trust also in me" (John 14:1 NLT). Complete trust in the One who loves us dispels anxiety. What peace! Second, Jesus will return and take us to live

81

with him forever (v. 3). What hope! Third, we know the way to his heavenly home (v. 4). What joy!

Jesus's answer to Thomas assures us of three more truths: Contrary to what some say, Jesus is the only means of access into God's presence. This access is available to us 24/7 once we have accepted him as Savior (Hebrews 4:15–16). He is also the source of all truth—not only about eternal life but also about earthly life. We rely on his teachings to help us navigate this world and to guide us into eternity (Psalm 119:105). Third, he is the only source of abundant, purposeful life on earth. Any other promised path of life is actually a road to destruction (Proverbs 14:12; Matthew 7:13).

Is something or someone obscuring your spiritual vision today? Focus on the truths Jesus gave in these verses. They'll provide the illuminating hope you need to dispel any fog that difficulty or doubt creates.

Reflections

_____

_____

_____

_____

_____

Dig Deeper

1. Read John 14:1–31. What other promises did Jesus give the disciples in this chapter? Which one means the most to you at this point in your life?

2. The disciples were upset that Jesus was "going away." But whose arrival was contingent on Jesus's departure according to John 16:7–15? Why did Jesus consider this arrival so vital for his disciples (and for us)?

3. Compare Jesus's words in John 14:6–7 with Peter's statements in Acts 2:32–36 and 4:8–12. How do these verses confirm that there is only one way to get to heaven?

Day 20
The Resurrection and the Life

Jesus said to [Martha], "I am the resurrection and the life. The one who believes in me will live, even though they die; and whoever lives by believing in me will never die. Do you believe this?" John 11:25–26

Shortly before his death and resurrection, Jesus performed an amazing miracle. When told that his dear friend Lazarus was ill, Jesus delayed two days before going to him (John 11:5–6). As he and his disciples headed to Judea, Jesus told them Lazarus was dead, then added, "And for your sake I am glad I was not there, so that you may believe" (John 11:15). His words and delay may seem heartless, but he knew what was going to happen.

Many people had come to console Lazarus's sisters, Mary and Martha. "Lord, if you had been here, my brother would not have died," Martha said after she greeted him. "But I know that even now God will give you whatever you ask" (John 11:21–22). Did she suspect what was going to happen?

When Jesus told her, "Your brother will rise again," she answered, "I know he will rise in the resurrection at the last day" (vv. 23–24).

"I am the resurrection and the life," Jesus said. "Whoever lives by believing in me will never die." He then challenged her commitment and asked, "Do you believe this?" (vv. 25–26).

"Yes, Lord," she replied (v. 27).

Mary and her friends came to him weeping. Jesus wept too. He loved Lazarus and his sisters. Even though Jesus was about to raise Lazarus from the dead, Jesus felt intense grief and anger—not only for these people but also for all the suffering that death brings into the world.

At the tomb, Jesus said, "Take away the stone" (v. 39). The mourners were reluctant to do so because Lazarus had been in the tomb four days, and, as Martha said, "by this time there is a bad odor" (v. 39).

Then the One who is The Life cried, "Lazarus, come out!" (v. 43). And the man who had died came out.

Soon Jesus would die on the cross. But the One who is The Resurrection would emerge from his tomb on the third day. Moreover, whoever believes in Jesus Christ will never die. Our bodies may die, but our lives are secure in the One who is The Resurrection and The Life.

Do you believe this? If so, your body may die, but you will have eternal life.

Reflections

_____

_____

_____

_____

_____

Dig Deeper

1. Read John 11:1–44. What was Jesus's response when he heard Lazarus was ill (v. 4)? Jesus knew Lazarus was going to die, so what did Jesus mean when he said, "this sickness will not end in death"?

2. Who is going to be resurrected? What are the two types of resurrection according to John 5:24–29?

3. Meditate on the significance of Christ's death and resurrection this Easter using Paul's description of what it means to be alive in Christ—Colossians 2:6–15. What parts of his description are especially meaningful to you?

Day 21
Lord of the Bent and Burdened

Jesus said, *"If the Son sets you free, you will be free indeed."* John 8:36

The woman needed a miracle, but she didn't ask for one. She may have cowered in the back of the synagogue, hoping no one would notice she'd come that day. After all, who wanted to look at a disfigured woman, bent over and unable to straighten up? (Luke 13:11).

But Jesus saw her, and he called her to come forward. "Woman," he said, "you are set free from your infirmity" (v. 12). And immediately she straightened her back and stood tall—something she hadn't done for eighteen years.

She rejoiced. Most of the crowd was delighted. But the Pharisees were indignant. "There are six days for work. So come and be healed on those days, not on the Sabbath," they said (v. 14).

Once again the Pharisees missed the point. Jesus, the Messiah, wasn't bound by the Pharisees' oppressive interpretations of the Mosaic law and their additions to it. Compassion motivated Jesus to challenge the legalistic burden the Pharisees had lain on every Jew.[12] And compassion compelled Jesus to remove the woman's physical burden that Sabbath day (v. 16).

Jesus came to set people free. Physical healings were visual signs of his power to free people from all that held them in bondage—especially the sin that separated them from God. As Peter explained on Pentecost, "Through [Jesus] everyone who believes is set free from every sin, a justification you were not able to obtain under the law of Moses" (Acts 13:39).

Are you, like the woman, cowering in the shadows—reluctant to ask Jesus to remove your burden? Have years of experience with people like the Pharisees made you think you're unworthy of Jesus's attention and undeserving of his love?

Don't focus on your burden or your critics. Look to Jesus. He's calling your name and beckoning you to come. Allow him to set you free and rekindle your hope. Then stand tall, rejoice, and share with others the life-transforming power and message of the Messiah.

Reflections

_____

_____

_____

_____

_____

Dig Deeper

1. Read Matthew 12:1–14. What did the Pharisees say about the Sabbath in this passage? What was Jesus's response?

2. Read Isaiah 42:1–7. How did Jesus fulfill these prophecies about the Messiah?

3. Read Romans 14:13–23. The Pharisees were so focused on dos and don'ts that they missed the salvation Jesus offered. What guidelines are given in this passage for handling disagreements about what Christians should and shouldn't do?

Day 22
The True Vine

Jesus said, *"I am the true vine, and my Father is the gardener. He cuts off every branch in me that bears no fruit, while every branch that does bear fruit he prunes so that it will be even more fruitful. ... I am the vine; you are the branches. If you remain in me and I in you, you will bear much fruit; apart from me you can do nothing."* John 15:1–2, 5

"I am the true vine," Jesus said. Perhaps he had in mind the vines in the vineyards he and his disciples passed as they journeyed to Jerusalem. Maybe he remembered the vine symbolic of Israel depicted on the temple they'd passed. Or as they ate, did he look at the cupful of wine on the table before him?

Jesus's words meant that he was not only the genuine vine but also the fulfillment of this symbol found in Scripture: "The vineyard of the Lord Almighty is the nation of Israel, and the people of Judah are the vines he delighted in. And [the Lord] looked for justice, but saw bloodshed; for righteousness, but heard cries of distress" (Isaiah 5:7). Unfortunately, Israel didn't bear the fruit God wanted.

But Jesus would bear fruit for God. Not natural children—but spiritual children—for when "the Lord makes his life an offering for sin, he will see his offspring" (Isaiah 53:10–11). Beginning with his disciples, Jesus's offspring were fruit-bearers. We are too.

Note that we're to *bear* fruit, not *produce* it. What's the difference? Jesus's mother, Mary, is an excellent example of a fruit-bearer. The angel told her, "You will conceive and give birth to a son, and you are to call him Jesus" (Luke 1:31). When Mary asked how a virgin could conceive, the angel said the Holy Spirit would come upon her (Luke 1:35). Mary couldn't produce a child by herself. She had to bear him—to accept, carry, give birth to him.

Jesus said we're unable to bear fruit apart from him (15:4–5). As part of vine life, we must stay connected to him. The Holy Spirit in us produces the fruit (Galatians 5:22–23). We accept, carry, and give birth to it.

God isn't asking you to produce fruit by your own efforts. Bear the fruit that's being produced in you as part of the vine. Stay connected.

Reflections

_____

_____

_____

_____

_____

Dig Deeper

1. What about branches that are cut off (John 15:2)? Can they be restored? Paul speaks of this in relation to Israel in Romans 11:22–24. What must happen before the gardener will graft the pruned branches back in again?

2. Read John 15:1–8. The gardener prunes us so that we'll be fruitful. See Galatians 5:16–21 for "branches" that need to be cut off. What is God pruning from your life?

3. Read Jude 1:20–25. How are we, as part of the vine, supposed to relate to others who are part of the vine?

Day 23
What Jesus Wants

The man said ... "To love [God] with all your heart, with all your understanding and with all your strength, and to love your neighbor as yourself is more important than all burnt offerings and sacrifice." Mark 12:33

As the time of his crucifixion drew near, Jesus spent many hours teaching at the temple. In the parable of the vineyard owner, he let the religious leaders know that he was aware of their murderous intentions and that they would be held accountable for their actions (Mark 12:1–12). Just as the tenant farmers disdained the owner's son in the parable, the religious leaders disdained Jesus, the Son of God. They didn't give to Jesus the respect, and therefore the worship, he deserved.

But Jesus's warning didn't stop the religious leaders. Instead, they sent more people to "catch him in his words" (Mark 12:13). And, as usual, Jesus turned their tricky questions into declarations of truth. After responding to three other questions in verses 13–34, Jesus asked a question designed to lead the religious leaders back to the truth of his identity.

In verses 35–37, Jesus referred to Psalm 110. Every Jew knew the Messiah would be David's descendant. That's why the people shouted, "Hosanna, to the Son of David" when Jesus entered the city a few days before his death (Matthew 21:9). Jesus wanted the religious leaders and the crowd to understand fully that the Messiah wasn't merely the Son of David. He was the Son of God.

97

In essence, Jesus asked, "Why would David call the Messiah, 'Lord,' if the Messiah were simply his biological son?" The nature of the question implies the answer: The Messiah isn't human. He's divine. He's David's Lord (*Yahweh*, the great I AM). The religious leaders knew what Jesus meant but refused to accept it.

Sometimes we sit piously in our pews and wonder how the religious leaders could've been so hard-hearted and hardheaded. Why didn't they recognize Jesus was the Son of God? And yet often we're no better than they. Like the tenant farmers in the parable, we don't respect or worship the Father's Son, our Master, as we should.

To each of us, Jesus says, "Loving me with all your heart is more important than any act of service you could offer." As his servants, our hearts and our lives, belong to him.

Will we give to God what is God's?

Reflections

_____

_____

_____

_____

_____

Dig Deeper

1. Study Jesus's interaction with the religious leaders in Mark 12:13–34. What is important to the religious leaders? What is more important to Jesus? As his servants, what should be important to us?

2. Contrast what Jesus says about the tenant farmers (vv. 7–9) and the scribes (vv. 38–40) with what he says about the widow (vv. 41–44). What would he say about you?

3. Read Romans 14:5–8 and 1 Corinthians 6:18–20. What practical applications of the principle "give to God what is God's" (Mark 12:17) are highlighted in these passages?

Part Three

The Last Week
Sunday to Saturday

Jesus took the Twelve aside and told them, "We are going up to Jerusalem, and everything that is written by the prophets about the Son of Man will be fulfilled. He will be delivered over to the Gentiles. They will mock him, insult him and spit on him; they will flog him and kill him. On the third day he will rise again."
Luke 18:31–33

Day 24
The Righteous One Comes

Open for me the gates of the righteous; I will enter and give thanks to the Lord. This is the gate of the Lord through which the righteous may enter. Psalm 118:19–20

Four days before the Passover feast, Jews brought an unblemished lamb into their homes—the lamb would become their atonement sacrifice (Exodus 12:3–6). Four days before his arrest, the Lamb of God entered the city of Jerusalem—the Lamb who would become the atonement sacrifice for all people.

Psalm 118 was definitely on Jesus's mind when he rode the donkey through the holy city. He heard the crowd shouting, "Blessed is he who comes in the name of the Lord" (118:26). Waving celebratory palm branches was a common practice during festal processions (v. 27). And Psalm 118 was one of six psalms customarily sung during Passover.[13]

As the crowd cheered, Jesus may have been thinking of verses 17–18: "I will not die but live and will proclaim what the Lord has done. The Lord has chastened me severely, but he has not given me over to death." Although Jesus would be slain as the atonement for sin, he also would rise again to eliminate forever the power of sin and the need for atonement. As Paul later wrote, "Death has been swallowed up in victory ... through our Lord Jesus Christ" (1 Corinthians 15:54, 57).

Jesus went directly to the temple after the procession (Mark 11:11). Did he look toward the Court of the Priests and think of the rest of Psalm 118:27: "With boughs in hand, join in the festal procession up to the horns of the altar"?[14] Each year, the blood of the Passover lamb was smeared on the horns of the altar (Leviticus 16:18–19). This year, Jesus was the lamb. This year, his blood would be shed.

Psalm 118 begins and ends with the refrain: "Give thanks to the Lord, for he is good; his love endures forever." Jews often sang this affirmation of God's steadfast love during feasts and other celebrations (see Ezra 3:11; Jeremiah 33:10–11). The psalmist used "his love endures forever" five times. The Lamb of God's voluntary entrance into the city where he would be crucified was a declaration of his love.

Although millions of people have entered Jerusalem's gates over the last 3,000 years, only One was truly righteous. And he loved us enough to become our savior (118:14). Will you sing of his everlasting goodness and love today?

Reflections

_____

_____

_____

_____

_____

Dig Deeper

1. Jews typically sang Psalms 113–118 during Passover, so Jesus probably sang them the night he was arrested. What verses in those psalms might have encouraged Jesus? Which verses encourage you?

2. The day after Jesus rode into Jerusalem, he quoted Psalm 118:22 in the temple. Read Matthew 21:33–46. Why did Jesus quote the verse? Why were the chief priests and Pharisees so upset?

3. Peter quoted Psalm 118:22 twice, in Acts 4:8–12 and 1 Peter 2:4–8. What point was he making in each instance?

Day 25
Our Father's Business

Jesus said, *"When you have lifted up the Son of Man, then you will know that I am he and that I do nothing on my own but speak just what the Father has taught me."* John 8:28

Four days to live. What would you be doing if you knew your time on earth was that short? Luke tells us that Jesus spent at least two of the days prior to his crucifixion in the temple, teaching the people and preaching the gospel (Luke 19:47; 20:1).

On Monday, Jesus drove the moneychangers out of the temple because they had defiled God's house by making it a "den of thieves" (Luke 19:46). The religious leaders demanded, "Tell us by what authority you are doing these things." Jesus defended his authority and his deity by telling the parable of the king whose son was rejected (Luke 20:1–8, Matthew 21:23–46).

On Tuesday, Jesus created verbal portraits of what genuine faith looked like in the parables of the Ten Virgins and the Talents (Matthew 25:1–30). With graphic illustrations, he showed people the disguises that falsehood and hypocrisy wore (Matthew 23:13–36; 25:31–46). He condemned the religious leaders' pride but praised a widow's humble generosity (Luke 20:45–21:4).

Jesus also challenged the crowd that gathered around him at the temple each day: Would they embrace him as the Son of David, their Divine Messiah, or would they reject him as a blaspheming imposter? (Luke 20:41–44).

Alone with the disciples on Tuesday night, Jesus spoke at length about the end times (Matthew 24:3–28; Luke 21:5–36). He advised them to be watchful—discerning, perceptive, and wary—of all teachings other than his own (Luke 21:8). He also said, "be careful"—exercise constant vigilance—for the "anxieties of life" might distract them from being ready when he returned (21:34).

I don't know if I have four days or 4,000 days left on earth. But Jesus says to me, to all of us, "Be always on the watch, and pray" (Luke 21:36). He spent every day diligently doing his Father's will. And so should we. In our words, deeds, and even in our thoughts we are to be "about [our] Father's business" (Luke 2:49 NKJV).

Are we heeding? Are we watching? Are we busy with the Father's business or our own?

Reflections

_____

_____

_____

_____

_____

Dig Deeper

1. Read Luke 2:41–49. Some versions of the Bible use "in my father's house" instead of "about my father's business" in verse 49. What was Jesus doing in his father's house according to this passage? What was he still doing in Luke 20–21? What business has your heavenly Father given you to do?

2. Contrast Jesus's words in Luke 21:36 with the disciples' actions in Luke 22:45–46. How often are you as "sleepy" as they were?

3. Read 1 Thessalonians 5:1–8 and 1 Peter 4:7–9. Besides being watchful and alert, what other characteristics should Christians manifest during the end times?

Day 26
A Celebration of God's Grace

And [Jesus] said to them, "I have eagerly desired to eat this Passover with you before I suffer. For I tell you, I will not eat it again until it finds fulfillment in the kingdom of God. . . . I will not drink again of the fruit of the vine until the kingdom of God comes." (Luke 22:15–16, 18)

We call the Last Supper *communion*, which comes from the Greek word *koinonia*, meaning "fellowship, partnership, or shared by all."[15] Jesus instituted this sacrament during the Passover meal he ate with his disciples before he was crucified.

Jews celebrated the Passover to commemorate God's deliverance of the Israelites from their Egyptian bondage. God had told Moses to commemorate yearly the Passover meal the Israelites had eaten before they left Egypt. On that night all the firstborn sons of the Egyptians died, but God "passed over" the firstborn sons of those who sacrificed a lamb and sprinkled its blood on their doorposts and lintel (Exodus 12:1–24).

Jesus knew that the last Passover he celebrated with his disciples would be more than a commemoration of something that happened centuries earlier. During the meal, he said, "This is my body given for you; do this in remembrance of me." After the supper, he took the cup and said, "This cup is the new covenant in my blood, which is poured out for you" (Luke 22:19–20).

Jesus also thought about the next time he would eat a celebratory meal with his disciples—not only the ones

111

gathered in the upper room that night. To that group would be added other disciples from every tribe and tongue and nation (Revelation 7:9). Jesus will wait until the kingdom comes in its fullness to drink again of the fruit of the vine.

Passover and communion are acts of worship that celebrate God's grace. He delivered his people from bondage through the blood that was shed—symbolically through the Passover lamb and ultimately through Jesus's death on the cross (Hebrews 9:12–15).

Communion looks back to Jesus's death as the Lamb of God, but it also looks forward to the Wedding Supper of the Lamb when the kingdom of God will come in its fullness (Revelation 19:7–9).

We wait in hope, knowing that we'll enjoy the glorious Wedding Supper of the Lamb. Can you imagine? We will eat the meal and drink wine with Jesus Christ!

Reflections

_____

_____

_____

_____

_____

Dig Deeper

1. Read Luke 19:11–26. Why did Jesus tell this parable? What were the people supposed to do while waiting for the return of the king? What should we be doing while we wait for his return?

2. In one of Jesus's parables, a guest was thrown out of the wedding celebration because he didn't have the garment provided for guests (Matthew 22:10–14). According to Isaiah 61:10, what garment should the wedding guest have been wearing?

3. Read Revelation 12:10–11. What are some things that happen when the kingdom of God comes fully? The word *fulfilled* in Luke 22:16 means "to make full, to fill to the top, fill to the brim, to consummate, to cause God's will (as made known in the law) to be obeyed as it should be, and God's promises (given through the prophets) to receive fulfillment."[16]

Day 27
The Covenant of Promise

In the same way, after the supper he took the cup, saying, "This cup is the new covenant in my blood, which is poured out for you." Luke 22:20

Do you ever feel like you just can't stop sinning? Many Christians feel that way. Maybe that's the reason some people buy this bumper sticker: Christians aren't perfect, just forgiven.

Israel had been chosen by God to be his special people, but they weren't perfect either. During the days of Moses, God established a covenant with the Israelites at Mount Sinai. The Ten Commandments were a part of that covenant (Deuteronomy 5:1–22).

The word *covenant* used in Luke is from a Greek word meaning "a testament, will, or covenant."[17] A covenant specifies relationships and responsibilities between two parties. According to one Bible dictionary, the most sacred covenant of all required that something or someone had to die—blood must be shed. Both parties pledged their lives: if the covenant was broken, the party breaking it must die.[18] Therefore, when the Israelites broke the covenant by turning their back on God and worshiping other gods, the terms of their agreement required a death.

When Jesus told his disciples at the Last Supper that he was about to die and pour out his blood for them, they didn't understand what he meant. Not until after his resurrection did they realize that his death was "a ransom to set them

115

free from the sins committed under the first covenant"—the Mosaic one (Hebrews 9:15).

The new covenant gives Christians imputed righteousness. *Imputed* means "credited, ascribed, given to another."[19] Christ's sinlessness and obedience was credited to us, and we've been declared righteous; however, we'll continue to commit sinful acts until we die because we're born with a sinful nature.

The new covenant is a covenant of promise. "Christ was sacrificed once to take away the sins of many; and he will appear a second time, not to bear sin, but to bring salvation to those who are waiting for him" (Hebrews 9:28).

Don't feel defeated because you sin. Trust Jesus Christ. His shed blood on the cross ratified the promises of the new covenant. Set your hope on the fact that his righteousness has permanently set you free from your bondage to sin.

Reflections

_____

_____

_____

_____

_____

Dig Deeper

1. Read Genesis 15:6–21. How was Abraham made righteous? How are you made righteous?

2. Read Romans 4:13–25. What message is given to us about imputed (credited) righteousness? How can those words give you hope when you've sinned—again?

3. Hebrews 12:18–24 says we haven't come to a terrifying Mount Sinai experience. What have we come to experience—now and in the future?

Day 28
The Call to Serve

Jesus said, *"I have set you an example that you should do as I have done for you."* John 13:15

Changing my children's diapers was often an unpleasant task, but I did it because I loved them. I'm not enthusiastic about cleaning bathrooms either—especially someone else's bathroom—but I do it willingly because I care about the people who use them.

On the night before his crucifixion, Jesus demonstrated his love for the disciples by undertaking the menial task of washing their feet (John 13:3–17). In doing so, he defined biblical servanthood.

John prefaces the story of our Savior's humble act by writing, "Jesus knew that the Father had put all things under his power, and he had come from God and was returning to God; so he got up from the meal ..." (13:3). The certainty of who he was and what he possessed enabled Jesus to serve others. He had nothing to prove and no pride to preen.

Knowing who we are in Christ enables us to serve without an agenda too. We are children of God and fellow heirs with Christ. The certainty of our identity in him and our home in heaven should fill us with so much love and gratitude that we seek opportunities to serve.

Peter misunderstood this kind of service. He assumed that such acts were signs of inferiority. That's why he objected so strongly: "You [Jesus] shall never wash my feet" (v. 8).

119

Jesus, however, was modeling mutual service. We serve each other as equals, as an outworking of our love for them and their love for us. Within the Christian community, there is neither servant nor master—not even elder brother and younger brother (v. 16).

Our culture, as well as our egos, resists mutual service. We typically look for a pecking order—hoping our status will place us in a more favorable position. But Jesus calls us to "wash one another's feet" (v. 14)—to embrace menial roles for his glory.

What act of service can you embrace this week? Working in your church's nursery, serving a meal in a homeless shelter, or cleaning bathrooms for an elderly person? If we serve as a manifestation of love, Jesus gives us this promise: "Now that you know these things, you will be blessed if you do them" (v. 17).

Reflections

_____

_____

_____

_____

_____

Dig Deeper

1. Read James 2:1–9. What counsel does James give about pecking orders in the church? How can we avoid that problem in our churches?

2. Read Luke 12:35–48. What does Jesus teach us about service in these two parables? What does the master do in the first parable to show his appreciation? Why do you think Jesus used such harsh language in the second parable?

3. Read Acts 6:1–4. What did the apostles say about serving tables? Did their actions conflict with Jesus's teaching in John 13? Why or why not?

Day 29
The Invitation to Abide

Jesus said, *"Abide in me, and I in you. Just as a branch cannot bear fruit by itself, unless it remains on the vine, neither can you unless you remain in me."* (John 15:4 ESV)

People don't use the word *abide* much anymore. It smells a little musty and looks a bit worn, like furniture in an antique store. But *abide* is the perfect word for describing the kind of relationship Jesus offered to his twelve disciples in the upper room—and to us.

Some modern translations use *remain* or *live* in John 15, but those words lack the intimacy, the hominess of *abide*. It's the difference between ordering room service in a five-star hotel room and settling in at Grandma's home for a week of her comfort-food meals served with soul-reviving hospitality. The warmth of a hand-stitched quilt, the aroma of freshly baked chocolate-chip cookies, the smooth leather cover of a well-read Bible—*abide* is that kind of word.

The Greek word translated *abide* can refer to place, time, or condition. According to Thayer's lexicon, it suggests an unbroken fellowship with someone. In reference to the Holy Spirit, it implies a relationship established "permanently in my soul," which "continually exerts power on me."[20]

Jesus used the metaphor of a grape vine and its branches to explain to the disciples the principle of abiding. Branches are only able to thrive and produce fruit if they're connected to the vine. Separated from the vine, the branches become fire fodder.

123

Similarly, we can do nothing of any eternal value—nothing that brings glory to Jesus—if we don't abide in him. The tendency to wander, to strike out on our own, is always a fruitless, unsatisfying, and often destructive venture.

A few hours after Jesus said, "Abide in me," the disciples chose not to abide. They fled into the darkness when the soldiers arrested the Lord. But the days of separation from Jesus—between his crucifixion and resurrection—cured the disciples of their wanderlust. After Jesus ascended into heaven, the disciples remained true. Through the power of the indwelling Spirit, they embraced the "abide in me" lifestyle until they were martyred.

We have that choice too. The King of Kings and Lord of Lords offers us the privilege of abiding in his presence, of taking up permanent residence with him, to enjoy all the blessings of his intimate companionship.

Will we accept his invitation?

Reflections

_____

_____

_____

_____

_____

Dig Deeper

1. Read Psalm 15. Some versions use "abide" in verse 1; others use "dwell." What are the characteristics of those who abide/dwell in God's presence? Ask the Holy Spirit to reveal to you how you can move toward meeting these standards of holiness.

2. Read Psalm 91. What are the blessings of abiding "in the shadow of the Almighty" (ESV) according to this psalmist?

3. Read John 12:24–26. What similarities do you see between the seed metaphor in this passage and the vine metaphor in John 15?

Day 30
"Ask in My Name"

Jesus said, *"And I will do whatever you ask in my name, so that the Father may be glorified in the Son. You may ask me for anything in my name, and I will do it."* John 14:13–14

If you could have three wishes fulfilled, what would you wish for? You may be reluctant to make three wishes if you remember the folktales about people whose third wish was to undo the first two wishes that hadn't turned out as they'd expected.

But in the upper room, Jesus told his disciples three times to ask him for anything and he would do it (John 14:13, 15:16, and 16:23–26). What was the condition of his promise? He'd do anything they asked "in my name." That would include anything they did as his deputies—anything he had authorized and anything he had instructed them to do.

Jesus said the disciples would do even greater things than the works they'd seen him do because he was going to the Father (v. 12). Jesus had raised the dead! How could the works of the disciples be greater than that?

Their works would be greater only in the sense that their works represented the actions of many people over thousands of years (so far) rather than Jesus's acts over the three years of his earthly ministry. The disciples would be his hands and feet on earth during his absence.

Jesus also told them to wait in Jerusalem for God to send the Holy Spirit (John 14:16–17). They waited and prayed.

On Pentecost, God poured out the Holy Spirit, and three thousand were added to the number of Jesus's followers (Acts 2:1–41).

Later, Peter and John went up to the temple at the time of prayer, and they prayed for a man who had been lame for forty years (Acts 4:22). He'd been carried to the temple gate every day to beg (Acts 3:2). Peter said to him, "Silver or gold I do not have, but what I do have I give you. In the name of Jesus Christ of Nazareth, walk" (3:6). And the man did walk. In fact, he walked into the temple courts and began "jumping and praising God" (3:8).

Peter boldly explained, "By faith in the name of Jesus, this man whom you see and know was made strong. It is Jesus's name and the faith that comes through him that has completely healed him, as you can all see" (Acts 3:16).

How's your faith? Do you boldly pray for things in the name of Jesus? Anything?

Reflections

_____

_____

_____

_____

_____

Dig Deeper

1. Read Genesis 3:1–6. What three wishes did the Serpent imply he would fulfill for Adam and Eve? Was the Serpent able to deliver on his promises? See Genesis 3:7–24, 4:8, and 5:5.

2. According to John 15:14–17, what did Jesus expect to see as the result of the disciples' prayers?

3. What were some other results of the disciples' prayers? See Acts 5:12–16. What has God authorized you to do in the name of Jesus?

Day 31
Fullness of Joy

Jesus said, *"I have told you this so that my joy may be in you, and that your joy may be complete."* John 15:11

According to the gospel accounts, Jesus talked more about joy on the night before his crucifixion than any other time during his earthly ministry. Does that seem odd to you?

In John 16:20, he told the disciples that they would soon weep, mourn, and grieve. Then he added that all their pain would be transformed into joy when they saw him again (v. 22). Jesus was talking about more than the sorrow they'd experience when he died and the joy they'd feel after his resurrection.

To understand Jesus's point, we may have to adjust our definition of joy. We often associate it with events—weddings, graduations, or other social gatherings. But Jesus told the disciples that their joy was connected to him and his teachings, not their circumstances.

For example, in John 15:9–11, Jesus connected joy to remaining in his love and obeying his commands. In John 17, Jesus again connected joy to his teachings. He said to God the Father, "I say these things while I am still in the world, so that [the disciples] may have the full measure of my joy within them" (v. 13). He summarized his teachings in verse 26: "I have made you [God the Father] known to them, and will continue to make you known in order that the love you have for me may be in them and that I myself may be in them."

This then is the joy of which Jesus spoke: We can know God. The more intimately we know him, the more joy we'll experience. How do we develop that intimacy? We give the Holy Spirit access to every part of our lives so he can "guide us into all the truth" (John 16:13). We "remain in [God's] love" (15:9) by spending time with him in prayer and Bible study. That will motivate us to obey his commands (15:10). The result is fullness of joy.

Do you long for the joy Jesus promised? I do. To receive it, we enter God's presence and open our hearts to receive his love. That's the first step toward experiencing the joy "no one will take away" (16:22).

Reflections

_____

_____

_____

_____

_____

Dig Deeper

1. Note what produces joy in these passages: Acts 8:5–8, Acts 13:49–52, and Acts 15:1–3. How are these things related to abiding in God's love and obeying his commands?

2. Read 1 John 1:3–4, 2 John 1:4, and 3 John 1:4. What does the apostle John associate with joy in these passages? Are those the things that fill your heart with joy as well?

3. Read 1 Peter 1:1–9 and 4:12–13. What does Peter say is related to fullness of joy?

Day 32
Appointed to Bear Fruit

Jesus said, *"You did not choose me, but I chose you and appointed you so that you might go and bear fruit—fruit that will last—and so that whatever you ask in my name the Father will give you."* John 15:16

Jesus's words to his disciples in the upper room remind me of a poem written by missionary C. T. Studd: "Only one life, 'twill soon be past / Only what's done for Christ will last."[21]

Many people have done good things, but how long did the fruit of their labor last after they died? They might have been very busy, but were they doing what God had appointed for them to do?

As Jesus gave final instructions to his disciples, he said he had chosen them. They'd spent time with the Master, witnessed his miracles, and heard his teachings. Soon he'd be gone. After he returned to heaven, they'd pray and see miracles happening around them; they'd teach and see God at work changing hearts. Jesus told them the Holy Spirit would come and live in them and remind them of what Jesus had said (John 14:16–17).

Then Jesus said something astonishing: It would be better if he went away, for if he didn't go away, the Comforter wouldn't come. But if he departed, he would send the Comforter to them (John 16:7).

Some versions say "it is better" in verse 7; some use the word *expedient*. How could it be better for Jesus to be absent? How could that be expedient? The Greek word in

135

John 16:7 is *symphero* and means "to bring together at the same time, or to help, to be profitable."[22] Think of a symphony where many instruments work together harmoniously. A symphonic orchestra couldn't be filled with only trumpets or only violins. The beautiful sound of an orchestra comes from many instruments each playing the part they've been appointed.

The word *appoint* can mean "ordain."[23] We might think of priests, ministers, or rabbis, who are ordained to work full time for God. But Jesus was sending out ordinary men—including fishermen and a tax collector. Not one of them was a learned scribe or a respected ruler of the synagogue (Acts 4:1–16). Each disciple would play a different part.

Do you know what God has appointed for you so you can produce lasting fruit for him? If not, ask in Jesus's name, and the Father will show you.

Reflections

_____

_____

_____

_____

_____

Dig Deeper

1. Read 1 Corinthians 12:4–27. Paul lists a variety of gifts and appointments that enable us to serve God. Paul then uses the human body to symbolize how Christians work together. What part of the body best represents your gifts and abilities—an arm, a mouth, a foot?

2. Compare the appointments given to the following people: Abraham in Genesis 12:1–3, Moses in Exodus 3:1–10, Isaiah in Isaiah 6:8–11, and Paul in Acts 9:1–15. How did the appointments differ? What lasting fruit did each person bear?

3. Read Psalm 1:1–3 and Psalm 92:12–15. How did the blessed ones become fruitful? How can you be more fruitful in your appointed walk with God?

Day 33
Seeing Our Weaknesses

"Simon, Simon, Satan has asked to sift all of you as wheat. But I have prayed for you, Simon, that your faith may not fail. And when you have turned back, strengthen your brothers." But he replied, "Lord, I am ready to go with you to prison and to death." Luke 22:31–33

Jesus loved Peter, formerly called Simon, even when he did foolish things. Peter often acted impulsively and sometimes wrongly.

Peter loved Jesus and didn't want him to die. He was willing to do whatever he could to prevent others from killing Jesus. When the chief priests, Pharisees, and officers of the temple guard came to arrest Jesus, the disciples saw what was going to happen and asked, "Lord, should we strike with our swords?" (Luke 22:49).

Peter didn't wait for an answer. He boldly drew his sword and struck Malchus, the high priest's servant, cutting off his right ear. But Jesus said, "No more of this!" He touched the man's ear and healed him (John 18:10 and Luke 22:50–51).

After Jesus was arrested and taken away, Peter followed at a distance. He was losing his courage. When faced with his own arrest in the temple courtyard, he weakened. Fear replaced zeal, and Peter denied he knew Jesus. Three times (Luke 22:54–61).

But Jesus is never surprised by our weaknesses. After Peter's third denial, Jesus turned and looked at Peter. Was his look full of compassion? Forgiveness? Love? It was not full of condemnation. Jesus had predicted Peter's denials and had prayed for him, saying, "When [not if] you've turned back, strengthen your brothers" (22:32–34).

Peter hadn't seen his weakness even when Jesus warned him about it at the Last Supper. Jesus had said to Peter, "Satan has asked to sift all of you as wheat" (Luke 22:31). But Jesus prayed for them (v. 32).

He prays for us too: "Because Jesus lives forever, he has a permanent priesthood. Therefore he is able to save completely those who come to God through him, because he always lives to intercede for them" (Hebrews 7:24–25).

Have you experienced Satan's sifting and succumbed to sin? Have you acted impulsively and done foolish things? Jesus is praying right now that your faith won't fail. Turn back. Jesus loves you. Trust him.

Reflections

_____

_____

_____

_____

_____

Dig Deeper

1. What weakness did James and John display in Mark 3:17 and Luke 9:51–56? What weakness do you struggle with most often?

2. Read Psalm 19:12–13. What are the two types of sin David asks God to forgive? Do you see both types in your life? According to the psalm, how can you be blameless?

3. Read 2 Corinthians 12:8–10. Why did Paul say he could boast and delight in his weaknesses? Do you have a weakness that causes you to sin? How often have you prayed about it? How can you boast and delight in this weakness rather than feel frustrated?

Day 34
Betrayed by a Friend

Yea, mine own familiar friend, in whom I trusted, which did eat of my bread, hath lifted up his heel against me. Psalm 41:9 (KJV)

Judas walked with Jesus for three years. He saw miracles, heard teachings—not only the public ones, but also the amplified versions Jesus taught his disciples in private. Judas ate and slept with the group. He was entrusted with the job of treasurer.

When Mary of Bethany anointed Jesus's feet, Judas asked, "Why wasn't this perfume sold and the money given to the poor? It was worth a year's wages" (John 12:5). Matthew records that Judas then went to the chief priests and asked what they'd give him to deliver Jesus. They offered him thirty pieces of silver, and "from then on Judas watched for an opportunity to hand him over" (Matthew 26:16).

Jesus knew from the beginning who would betray him (John 6:64), but he never treated Judas differently than he treated the other disciples. At the Last Supper, Jesus placed Judas in the honored spot next to himself. He washed Judas's feet knowing what Judas was about to do.

When Jesus said, "one of you is going to betray me," the disciples "stared at one another, at a loss to know which of them he meant" (John 13:21–22). Some thought Jesus was sending Judas on an errand since he had charge of the money (13:29). They didn't know he'd been stealing from them.

John, who leaned against his Savior, noted that Jesus was "troubled in spirit" (John 13:21). He heard Jesus quote "he lifted his heel against me" (from Psalm 41:9). David wrote that psalm after his trusted adviser and friend, Ahithophel, joined David's son Absalom's revolt. To "lift your heel" was an idiom borrowed from kicking "or from a wrestler tripping up his antagonist."[24]

In another psalm, David wrote, "If an enemy were insulting me, I could endure it; if a foe were rising against me, I could hide. But it is you, a man like myself, my companion, my close friend, with whom I once enjoyed sweet fellowship at the house of God, as we walked about among the worshipers" (Psalm 55:12–14). Jesus also endured the scorn of his enemies, and he felt the pain of betrayal from one who had been close.

Have you been betrayed by a close friend? Jesus understands. Will you respond as compassionately as he did?

Reflections

_____

_____

_____

_____

_____

Dig Deeper

1. According to John 13:2 and 13:27, what happened because of Judas's decisions? What's the significance of John's comment in verse 30?

2. Although the disciples didn't understand at the time, how did Jesus's obvious foreknowledge of what was going to happen increase their faith later when they remembered his words? See John 13:2, 10–11, 18–19, and 26. In what ways do these words strengthen your faith and nourish your hope?

3. Do you think David's words in Psalms 41 and 55 were prophetic? Did the Spirit prompt him to say these things that Jesus would later say, or did Jesus just identify with David's feelings of betrayal? Consider what Jesus said in Luke 24:44.

Day 35
Would You Remain Silent?

"You are a king, then!" said Pilate. Jesus answered, "You say that I am a king. In fact, the reason I was born and came into the world is to testify to the truth. Everyone on the side of truth listens to me." John 18:37

In trial courts in the USA, a witness or defendant may say, "I plead the fifth." The Fifth Amendment of our constitution guarantees us the right to remain silent rather than incriminate ourselves.

Reading the accounts of Jesus's trials before the religious leaders and the political leaders, I was struck at first by his silence. Even though Jesus was falsely accused, he didn't defend himself. The One who said he came to testify to the truth knew those liars wouldn't listen to him.

But before an assembly of the high priest, all the chief priests, the elders, and the scribes, Jesus's words were not only truthful but also self-incriminating (Mark 14:53–62). The high priest asked Jesus to answer *under oath*, "Are you the Messiah, the Son of the Blessed One?" (v. 61).

Jesus said, "I am." He then added words from Scripture which were messianic: "And you will see the Son of Man sitting at the right hand of the Mighty One, and coming on the clouds of heaven" (Mark 14:62, quoting from Psalm 110:1 and Daniel 7:13–14).

In Psalm 110, David spoke of One he called "my Lord," who sat at the right hand of "the Lord" (Jehovah). Daniel described a heavenly court where books were opened and

147

judgment administered. One day Jesus will judge the men who judged him at his trials.

The Jewish religious court decided that Jesus had incriminated himself: he was guilty of blasphemy, punishable by death. Later Pilate, the Roman governor, asked Jesus, "Are you the king of the Jews?" Jesus answered, "You have said so" (Mark 15:2). Incriminating words: only Caesar was regarded as king—Jesus was guilty of treason, punishable by death. Although he believed Jesus was innocent, Pilate chose to appease the crowd. He released the insurrectionist, Barabbas, and then delivered Jesus to be crucified.

Hebrews 12:2 says that Jesus, "for the joy set before him ... endured the cross, scorning its shame, and sat down at the right hand of the throne of God." How would you respond if you were on trial for your faith? Would you say, "I plead the fifth"? Or would you courageously declare, as many others have, "I am a Christian"?

Reflections

_____

_____

_____

_____

_____

Dig Deeper

1. According to Mark 14:53–62, Mark 15:1–2, and John 18:36–37, what did Jesus say about himself? Who is he?

2. Read Matthew 14:1–12, Mark 6:14–29, and Luke 23:7–12. Why do you think Jesus was silent before Herod? Why do you think Herod and Pilate became friends after this?

3. James wrote, "No man can tame the tongue" (see James 3:1–12). But Jesus had power over his tongue. How could his example help you when you're falsely accused?

Day 36
At What Cost?[25]

He himself bore our sins in his body on the cross, so that we might die to sins and live for righteousness. 1 Peter 2:24

Three hundred years before Mel Gibson produced *The Passion of the Christ*, Isaac Watts wrote the lyrics of "When I Survey the Wondrous Cross." The third stanza, in particular, graphically portrays the cost of the cross: "See, from his head, his hands, his feet, Sorrow and love flow mingled down."

This image, simultaneously beautiful and repulsive, has brought tears to the eyes of devout Christians for centuries. Stirring our emotions, however, was not Watts's primary purpose for writing this hymn.

Watts concluded his meditation on the magnitude of Christ's love for sinners by saying, "Love so amazing, so divine, Demands my soul, my life, my all." And those words make a profound point: God never intended for us to simply cry over Christ's suffering. Gibson's movie motivated thousands of people to mourn the agony Jesus endured. However, they still walked out of the theaters without accepting him as Savior and Lord.

Unfortunately, my response to Christ's suffering is sometimes more like the movie theater crowd's than I like to admit. I am moved but not changed. I am sorrowful but not repentant. Singing "When I Survey the Wondrous Cross" should be more than an exercise in remembrance. It should convict me and humble me.

151

If Jesus's sacrifice does not call me to repentance and obedience, then it has not truly affected me, no matter how many tears I shed. The apostle Paul said it this way: "I consider everything a loss because of the surpassing worth of knowing Christ Jesus my Lord" (Philippians 3:8).

When we truly survey the cross and kneel in awe before the amazing love that was poured out there, it alters the way we live. We too will "consider everything a loss" except for an increasing devotion to the Prince of Glory who shed his blood for us.

As you sing the hymns of Easter this year, pay close attention to the lyrics and evaluate whether Jesus's death and resurrection have altered the way you live each day.

Reflections

_____

_____

_____

_____

_____

Dig Deeper

1. Read Psalm 22. Verses 1–18 give a graphic description of crucifixion that David wrote hundreds of years before the Romans ever implemented this cruel means of execution. What should be our response to Christ's death according to verses 27–31?

2. Paul advises us to "count ourselves dead to sin" in Romans 6:11–14. How can we do that? He gives a practical answer in Romans 12:9–16.

3. What kind of things did Paul count as "loss"? Read Philippians 3:3–5. What did he seek instead? Read Philippians 3:10.

"When I Survey the Wondrous Cross"
Isaac Watts, 1707, public domain

When I survey the wondrous cross
On which the Prince of glory died,
My richest gain I count but loss,
And pour contempt on all my pride.

Forbid it, Lord, that I should boast
Save in the death of Christ, my God!
All the vain things that charm me most,
I sacrifice them through his blood.

See, from his head, his hands, his feet,
Sorrow and love flow mingled down.
Did e'er such love and sorrow meet,
Or thorns compose so rich a crown?

Were the whole realm of nature mine,
That were a present far too small.
Love so amazing, so divine,
Demands my soul, my life, my all.

Day 37
Courage to Speak Boldly

And we have seen and testify that the Father has sent his Son to be the Savior of the world. If anyone acknowledges that Jesus is the Son of God, God lives in them, and they in God. 1 John 4: 14–15

Joseph of Arimathea was a prominent member of the Sanhedrin, the Jewish high council. His wealth and education had given him both power and prestige. He was also a disciple of Jesus (John 19:38). Maybe he'd stood in the crowds near the temple, at first as skeptical as his fellow council members. Perhaps, like Nicodemus, he'd come to Jesus under the cloak of darkness to question, learn, and believe.

Somewhere, somehow, his curiosity was transformed into conviction—a certainty that Jesus was the Messiah for whom he waited. However, Joseph "feared the Jews" so he kept his discipleship a secret (John 19:38).

Luke records that the "entire council" took Jesus to Pilate, so Joseph most likely was present when the religious leaders accused Jesus of "leading our people astray" (23:1–2 NLT). But apparently Joseph didn't attempt to defend Jesus. How did he feel when Pilate released Jesus into the custody of the murderous crowd (v. 25)?

After Jesus's death, Joseph couldn't remain silent any longer. He boldly went to Pilate and asked for Jesus's body. The bodies of state criminals were the property of the Roman government. Often they were cast in mass graves.

157

Joseph refused to allow Jesus's body to be desecrated that way.

Joseph's prestige and wealth enabled him to do what the twelve disciples couldn't have done. He gained access to Pilate who released Jesus's body into his custody. Then Joseph purchased costly linen (for wrapping the body). Nicodemus, another council member, brought the expensive embalming ointments. Together, they prepared Jesus's body for burial and placed him in a tomb Joseph had purchased (Luke 23:50–54).

After Jesus rose from the dead, did he seek out Joseph? Did he give Joseph a big hug and thank him for his bold actions? I like to think he did. After all, our Good Shepherd is quick to forgive his sheep when we disappoint him and quick to encourage us when we do what is right.

Sometimes, like Joseph, I keep silent when I should speak up. Maybe you do too. Do those missed opportunities prompt us to speak boldly the next time? I don't want to be a secret disciple. I want to embrace second chances as Joseph did, to obey the Spirit's promptings, and to tell others that I am a disciple of Jesus. Is that your desire as well?

Reflections

_____

_____

_____

_____

_____

Dig Deeper

1. Take time to read the Scriptures about Joseph of Arimathea this week and ask God to give you the boldness he gave to Joseph. Read Matthew 27:57–60, Mark 15:42–46, Luke 23:50–53 and John 19:38–42.

2. Read more about Nicodemus in John 3:1–21. Did Jesus scold him for coming secretly? What was Jesus's rebuke in verses 10–12? What was Jesus most concerned about that night?

3. The Greek word translated "acknowledges" in 1 John 4:15 ("confesses" in the KJV) means to "declare openly, to speak freely."[26] How can you acknowledge your faith in Jesus Christ this week?

Day 38
Light for the Dark Days

Jesus said, *"I have come into the world as a light, so that no one who believes in me should stay in darkness."* John 12:46

My husband, Ken, and I once took an overnight cruise to Nova Scotia. We boarded the ship just before sunset. When we'd sailed far from the harbor, I was struck by the sky's intense blackness. We saw nothing beyond the soft lights on the deck.

We awoke to a white fog in the morning. In a way, that whiteness was like the darkness of the previous night. Normally, daylight helps us to see, but that foggy day revealed nothing but whiteness. I was glad the boat's pilot had instruments to warn him of what he couldn't see and to indicate the right way to go.

While Jesus was dying on the cross, the sky was dark as night from noon until three in the afternoon. As his lifeless body was removed from the cross and placed in a tomb, his followers must have felt the darkness creep into their souls. The daylight returned after three o'clock, but the darkness remained in their hearts.

We can only imagine what the disciples experienced between Friday and Sunday. Memories of promises Jesus had made to them were blotted out by grief.

When the world around us seems to grow darker and darker each day with sinfulness and evil, we may experience a spiritual darkness similar to the grief and bewilderment Jesus's followers felt after he had died. We may feel like

161

the passengers on that boat in Nova Scotia—engulfed by the dark of night or a blinding morning fog. But like the pilot of that boat, we have a guiding instrument. God placed the Holy Spirit in us to warn us of what we cannot see and to tell us the right way to go.

Do we let the darkness overwhelm us, or do we rely on the Holy Spirit? While we see much darkness around us, we must place our unwavering hope in the promise of glorious light to come.

Reflections

_____

_____

_____

_____

_____

Dig Deeper

1. Read John 12:35–38. What does Jesus call those who put their trust in the light? How does he describe those who choose to walk in the darkness? How can we tell if we are walking in the light?

2. According to Psalm 139:11–12, what can give us hope when we are tempted to feel overwhelmed by the darkness?

3. What did Jesus tell his disciples about his imminent death in Matthew 17:22–23 and 20:17–19? What additional promises does Jesus make about the future in Matthew 16:21–27?

Part Four

Resurrection and Glory
Sunday and Evermore

*Now to him who is able to do immeasurably more
than all we ask or imagine, according to his power
that is at work within us, to him be glory in the church
and in Christ Jesus throughout all generations,
for ever and ever! Amen.*
Ephesians 3:20–21

Day 39
From Confusion to Confidence

"Don't be alarmed," [the angel] said . . . "He has risen! He is not here" . . . Trembling and bewildered, the women went out and fled from the tomb. Mark 16:6, 8

Flabbergasted—"overwhelmed with shock, surprise, or wonder."[27] Can any other word so accurately describe the emotional state of Jesus's followers as they witnessed his crucifixion on Friday, grieved his death on Saturday, then attempted to process his resurrection on Sunday?

Jesus tried to prepare them for the tsunami-force emotional onslaught they experienced those three days. Mark records Jesus's numerous declarations of what would occur (see Mark 8:31; 9:2, 31; 10:33–34, 45; 14:28). Yet his followers remained completely unprepared. Thus they grieved for him, stumbling around in the rubble of their faith, flummoxed by the devastation, and flabbergasted by its implications. And when they were confronted with the truth of his resurrection, they trembled with fear and wallowed in disbelief (Mark 16:5–6, 8, 11–14).

Neither the angels at the tomb nor Jesus himself excused his followers' disbelief. "Remember how he told you, while he was still with you in Galilee?" the angels chided (Luke 24:6). Later, in the room where many had gathered, Jesus said, "Why are you troubled, and why do doubts rise in your mind?" (Luke 24:38). It had all been too bad to be accepted; then suddenly it was all too good to comprehend.

Jesus wanted his followers to become fruitful servants and spread the gospel worldwide. That wasn't possible unless

167

they overcame their fear and doubt and embraced what had happened. So he opened the Scriptures to them (Luke 24:44–48). But not until the Holy Spirit came were they empowered to do the work he had assigned them (Luke 24:49; Acts 1:8).

We too are confronted with situations that may seem either too bad or too good to comprehend. We need the same thing the first-century followers needed: a personal encounter with the risen Christ, who alone can open our eyes to the truth of his Word, fill us with hope, and empower us by his Spirit to spread the gospel to others.

Feeling flabbergasted? Enter the presence of the risen Christ through prayer and ask him to lead you out of confusion and into confidence. His empty tomb testifies to his power to do anything for us, in us, and through us. Rejoice!

Reflections

_____

_____

_____

_____

_____

Dig Deeper

1. Read Mark 16:1–14. Imagine the roller coaster of emotions Jesus's followers experienced that day. What did he say to the eleven disciples in verse 14? Why do you suppose he responded that way?

2. Despair threatens all of us at some point. How did David move from despair to joy in Psalm 13?

3. How can the implications of Jesus's resurrection empower you to live in hope each day? Consider the truths Charles Wesley focused on in "Christ the Lord Is Risen Today." What would you add to his list?

Christ the Lord Is Risen Today
Charles Wesley, 1739, public domain

Christ the Lord is ris'n today, Alleluia!
Sons of men and angels say, Alleluia!
Raise your joys and triumphs high, Alleluia!
Sing, ye heav'ns, and earth, reply, Alleluia!

Lives again our glorious King, Alleluia!
Where, O death, is now thy sting? Alleluia!
Once He died our souls to save, Alleluia!
Where thy victory, O grave? Alleluia!

Love's redeeming work is done, Alleluia!
Fought the fight, the battle won, Alleluia!
Death in vain forbids His rise, Alleluia!
Christ hath opened paradise, Alleluia!

Soar we now where Christ hath led, Alleluia!
Foll'wing our exalted Head, Alleluia!
Made like Him, like Him we rise, Alleluia!
Ours the cross, the grave, the skies, Alleluia!

Hail the Lord of earth and heaven, Alleluia!
Praise to Thee by both be given, Alleluia!
Thee we greet triumphant now, Alleluia!
Hail the Resurrection, thou, Alleluia!

King of glory, Soul of bliss, Alleluia!
Everlasting life is this, Alleluia!
Thee to know, Thy pow'r to prove, Alleluia!
Thus to sing, and thus to love, Alleluia!

Day 40
Compelled by Love

All those who knew him, including the women who had followed him from Galilee, stood at a distance, watching these things. Luke 23:49

The women who ministered to Jesus and his disciples during the three years he traveled throughout Palestine were a diverse group. Matthew lists Mary Magdalene, Mary the mother of James and Joses, and also the unnamed mother of James and John (27:56). Mark names Salome and says that "many other women" had come to Jerusalem that week (Mark 15:40–41). John includes Mary, the wife of Clopas (John 19:25). Most likely, Joanna and Susanna were also in Jerusalem (see Luke 8:3).[28] The women came from different social strata. Some were the wives and mothers of fishermen. Joanna was married to King Herod's steward. A few were financially independent; Luke records that they supported Jesus's ministry "out of their own means" (Luke 8:3).

Luke also identifies the thread that bound the women together—Jesus had freed them from either disease or demons (Luke 8:2). Gratitude motivated them to serve their Savior. They probably fixed the meals, washed and mended clothes, fetched water, purchased food—doing whatever they could to make Jesus's ministry possible.

How great their sorrow must have been as they watched the crucifixion. On that horrific day, did they say to one another, "How can it end like this? How could we have been so wrong about Jesus?" Even if they doubted, they kept vigil until the soldiers took Jesus down from the cross.

173

Then they followed Joseph of Arimathea and Nicodemus to the tomb (Luke 23:55). Compelled by their steadfast love for Jesus, they purchased spices and went to the tomb early Sunday morning—as soon as the Sabbath laws permitted them to do so (Luke 23:56–24:1).

How spectacularly was their devotion rewarded! They saw the empty tomb before anyone else. They first heard the glorious news: "He is not here; he is risen!" (Luke 24:6). They hurried to tell others that Jesus had risen—just as he said (24:8–10, Matthew 28:8).

These women are such worthy role models. They humbly served their Savior in the most menial tasks because they loved him and wanted to be near him. Even when it seemed that their service had been futile, they still served him, still loved him.

Oh, that our love would be as selfless as theirs and our devotion as steadfast. Jesus has freed us from the most fatal disease—sin. He has delivered us from the power of every evil influence that can separate us from him. He has given us love, joy, and hope that no one can take away from us. May we be as quick to show our love for our risen Savior as the women of Galilee were.

Reflections

Dig Deeper

1. Read Luke 24:1–12. Who told the women Jesus had risen from the dead? What was their response? How did the disciples respond when the women told them about Jesus's resurrection? How do you think you would have responded?

2. Jesus told his followers repeatedly that he would both die and be resurrected: Matthew 16:21; 17:9, 23; 20:19; 26:32. Why didn't they remember according to Luke 18:32–34? What prevents you from remembering Jesus's promises in times of sorrow and disappointment?

3. What did Jesus say about the cost of serving him in Luke 9:23–27? What will be our reward if we serve him as faithfully as the women of Galilee did?

Day 41
Are You Slow of Heart?

Jesus said, *"Now is your time of grief, but I will see you again and you will rejoice, and no one will take away your joy."* John 16:22

Cleopas and his companion were devastated. Walking from Jerusalem to Emmaus, they discussed Passover week's tragic events and mourned the death of Jesus of Nazareth.

Then a stranger joined them and asked the reason for their sorrow. Because the man seemed eager to hear the story, they explained the treachery of the chief priests and rulers, the horror of the crucifixion, and the wild tales of the women who had visited the tomb.

But instead of murmuring condolences, the stranger said, "How foolish you are, and how slow of heart to believe all that the prophets have spoken!" (Luke 24:25). Although the Bible doesn't tell us how the travelers responded to Jesus's words, they probably were a little surprised by his rebuke.

Why did Jesus react that way? Why didn't he ooze sympathy or identify himself immediately? Jesus gave the answer himself: his companions were "slow of heart." In Greek, that phrase implies that a person's intellect is inactive or dull; in other words, the person isn't "connecting the dots."[29]

What dots were Cleopas and his companion supposed to connect? Jesus answered that too—"all that the prophets had spoken." For three years, Jesus had emphasized that he came to fulfill the prophecies recorded in the Scriptures (e.g. Mark 9:11–13). He told the twelve disciples

177

specifically that he would die and would rise again three days later (Mark 10:32–34). In Jerusalem, he reminded all who gathered around him that he would be lifted up to die (John 12:32–36).

Most of Jesus's followers were "slow of heart." If they had listened carefully, they would've been prepared, not only for the crucifixion but also for the resurrection! Their sorrow would have been tempered by their confident hope in Jesus's ultimate triumph over death.

How many of us make a similar mistake? We listen to some but not all of Jesus's words. Then when catastrophe strikes, we tumble into doubt and disappointment instead of clinging to the certainty that he has not forsaken us.

Jesus doesn't want any of us to be "slow of heart." He longs for us to know and digest "all the prophets have spoken" and everything the Scriptures say "concerning himself" (Luke 24: 25–27).

What steps can you take this week to develop a more attentive heart?

Reflections

_____

_____

_____

_____

_____

Dig Deeper

1. Read Luke 24:13–49. What strikes you most about Jesus's conversation with Cleopas and his companion? Would you have been quicker to recognize him? Why?

2. Not all of Jesus's followers were "slow of heart." Read John 12:3–7. How did this follower develop a discerning heart? Read Luke 10:38–42.

3. What reassurance did Jesus give the disciples in Mark 14:26–31? What were they thinking about? How was their focus different from Jesus's focus?

Day 42
The Message of the Scars

He said to them, "Why are you troubled, and why do doubts rise in your minds? Look at my hands and my feet. It is I myself! Touch me and see; a ghost does not have flesh and bones, as you see I have." Luke 24:38–39

When Jesus appeared to the disciples after his resurrection, he didn't knock at the locked door. His resurrection body was different because he did not enter the room through the door at all. He came through it or through the wall.

The disciples thought they were seeing a ghost, but Jesus reassured them that he was flesh and bones. The risen Jesus was not a ghost, not a "force," or a feeling. To reassure the disciples that he was the man they had known, Jesus showed them the scars on his hands, feet, and side. His resurrection body had scars.

What is the message of his scars? He's more than a man. He's the second person of the Trinity: Father, Son, and Holy Spirit. Only the death of the sinless Son of God could atone for our sins.

Jesus encouraged the disciples to study what had been written about him in the Scriptures: "This is what I told you while I was still with you: Everything must be fulfilled that is written about me in the Law of Moses, the Prophets and the Psalms" (Luke 24:44). What is the message we're given about Jesus Christ in the Bible? We have the Scriptures the disciples had and more—the Old and New Testaments. These Scriptures tell us who Jesus is, why he came to earth, and what he wants us to do.

Jesus told the disciples that repentance and forgiveness of sins would be preached in his name to all nations. "You are witnesses of these things" (Luke 24:47–48). What is the message we're to proclaim? We're witnesses of the repentance and forgiveness we've received in his name and ambassadors of the hope that the gospel message proclaims.

Jesus also told the disciples that he was going to send the Holy Spirit to them as the Father had promised: "But stay in the city until you have been clothed with power from on high" (Luke 24:49). What is the message of this promise for us? We too are to go out clothed with the power of the Holy Spirit.

Have you personally received these messages from the risen Christ? He still bears the scars that tell of his victory over sin and death. The Bible reveals Jesus's identity and his mission—past, present, and future. It reveals our identity and mission too. We are his disciples and his witnesses. Jesus Christ has given us the power of the Holy Spirit so that we might tell others of the victory over sin and death we've received.

Reflections

_____

_____

_____

_____

_____

Dig Deeper

1. Read Revelation 5:6. How does the apostle John symbolically describe the risen Christ? Why do you think Jesus has chosen to bear forever the scars of the crucifixion?

2. Read Psalm 69. What references to Jesus's suffering on the cross do you see in these words David wrote hundreds of years before Jesus came to earth?

3. All Jesus's disciples were persecuted, put to death, or exiled because of their witness. Read Matthew 10:16–28 and John 21:17–19. Have you been persecuted because of your witness or threatened with death? What are the warnings and reassurances Jesus offers us in these verses?

Day 43
Believe and Be Blessed

Jesus said, *"Because you have seen me, you have believed; blessed are those who have not seen me and yet have believed."* John 20:29

I've never liked nicknames. Because I was small for my age, peers often called me "small fry" and "shrimp." I've never liked the nicknames people give Bible characters either. For centuries, one of Jesus's disciples has been labeled "Doubting Thomas." True, he didn't believe that the other disciples had seen the risen Lord, but they had been equally skeptical before they saw him.

All the disciples had forgotten Jesus's declarations that he'd be resurrected. In fact, when the women declared the tomb was empty, the disciples considered their words "nonsense" (Luke 24:11). Their doubts were erased when Jesus entered a room even though the doors were locked. When Thomas saw Jesus, he too believed. He didn't need to touch him to know he was real. He immediately proclaimed, "My Lord and my God!" (John 20:28).

His declaration of Jesus's identity is a powerful testimony. The word translated "Lord" is *kyrios*—the Greek equivalent of two Hebrew words—*Jehovah* and *Adonai*. The word translated "God" is the Greek equivalent of *Elohim*. By saying "My Lord and my God" Thomas affirmed three truths: Jesus is *Jehovah*, the one true God of the Old Testament. He's *Adonai*, the owner and master of all people, and he is also *Elohim*, the triune creator and sovereign of the universe.[30]

185

Like some of the other disciples, Thomas had been following Jesus, the teacher and prophet. But Thomas's encounter with the resurrected Jesus convinced him that Jesus was more than a teacher, more than a prophet. Jesus was God in human form—worthy to be worshiped, not just followed.

Jesus rebuked Thomas for his lack of faith: "Stop doubting and believe" (John 20:27). I wonder if he'd say something similar to me. Sometimes my prayers express a similar "show me first" attitude: "Do this, Lord, and I will believe. Answer this way, and I will obey." Jesus may respond to such flimsy faith as he did in Thomas's case. But that's not the kind of faith that pleases him most.

Jesus said, "Blessed are those who have not seen and yet have believed" (v. 29). Are we willing to say "My Lord and my God" even when we can't see him? That is the true test of our commitment to the resurrected Christ.

Reflections

_____

_____

_____

_____

_____

Dig Deeper

1. Compare Thomas's declaration in John 20:28 with John's declarations both at the beginning and end of his book (John 1:14, John 20:30–31). Why are these statements so crucial to our understanding of who Jesus is?

2. Read Luke 24:1–12. Why do you think the disciples doubted the women's words? What is Peter's reaction? Why don't we call him "Doubting Peter"?

3. Who was Jesus talking about when he said "those who have not seen"? Consider John 8:56 and 1 Peter 1:8–9.

Day 44
The Forgiven Fisherman

Peter replied, "Repent and be baptized, every one of you, in the name of Jesus Christ for the forgiveness of your sins. And you will receive the gift of the Holy Spirit. The promise is for you and your children and for all who are far off—for all whom the Lord our God will call." Acts 2:38–39

"We found the Messiah," Andrew told Peter and then brought his brother to Jesus (John 1:41). But Peter went back to his job as a fisherman. One day Jesus told him to lower his nets for a catch. Peter protested, "Master, we've worked hard all night and haven't caught anything. But because you say so, I will let down the nets" (Luke 5:5). Astonished at the catch of fish that threatened to break their nets, the fishermen signaled their partners in another boat to help.

Peter then fell at Jesus's knees saying, "Go away from me, Lord; I am a sinful man!" But Jesus said, "Don't be afraid; from now on you will catch men." Peter left everything and followed Jesus (Luke 5:8–11).

After Jesus's death and resurrection, Peter probably felt that Jesus had no need of a fearful man who had three times denied knowing him, so Peter returned to fishing again. One morning, after a night of not catching anything, he and his companions saw a man on the shore.

"Friends, haven't you any fish?" the stranger asked. "Throw your nets on the other side of the boat" (John 21:5–6). When they were unable to haul in the net because of the large number of fish, John cried, "It is the Lord!" (v. 7).

189

Peter may have remembered the other time Jesus had given them such an incredible catch of fish. Hope stirred within the humbled fisherman. He jumped overboard and swam ashore.

Jesus had built a fire on the sand. The flames may have reminded Peter of the night he had warmed himself in the high priest's courtyard and denied that he knew Jesus three times. This time as Peter warmed himself by the fire, Jesus asked him, "Do you love me?" Three times Peter replied that he loved him. "Then feed my sheep," Jesus said, reminding Peter of his call to become a fisher of men (see Matthew 4:19; John 21:15–17). Jesus hadn't given up on him. Peter's hope blazed into commitment as the risen Christ reaffirmed the fisherman's call to service.

Sometimes when we fail to act as we should, we're tempted to think that Jesus might give up on us. But he knows our weaknesses and forgives our failures.

We can place our hope in his unfailing love. He will never give up on us.

Reflections

_____

_____

_____

_____

_____

Dig Deeper

1. Read Luke 22:31–34 and John 18:12–27. What details show that Jesus knew ahead of time that Peter would deny him?

2. Read John 21:1–19. What details show that Jesus planned ahead of time to forgive and reinstate Peter as a "fisher of men"?

3. Read Acts 2:14–41. Peter later overcame his fear and became a fisher of men as Jesus predicted. In Acts 2:38–39, Peter ended his first sermon with a plea to receive forgiveness for sins. How did the audience respond?

Day 45
"Why Do You Stand Here?"

When [Jesus] had led them out to the vicinity of Bethany, he lifted up his hands and blessed them. While he was blessing them, he left them and was taken up into heaven.
Luke 24:50–51

After the resurrection, Jesus appeared to the disciples over a period of forty days, opening their minds to what the Scriptures said about him and about the kingdom of God. One day, he led them to the vicinity of Bethany, to the Mount of Olives.

"Then they gathered around him and asked him, 'Lord, are you at this time going to restore the kingdom to Israel?'" (Acts 1:6–7). They were aware something was about to happen. They knew many Old Testament prophecies described the spiritual and national restoration of Israel. Would that happen soon because Jesus had risen from the dead?

He answered them, "It is not for you to know the times or dates the Father has set by his own authority. But you will receive power when the Holy Spirit comes on you; and you will be my witnesses in Jerusalem, and in all Judea and Samaria, and to the ends of the earth" (Acts 1:7–8).

Next on God's agenda would be sending the Holy Spirit who'd live inside them. Then they would go out as they had earlier "in Jesus's name" to witness, heal, and work miracles (Luke 10:1–24). They would make disciples, teaching all that Jesus had commanded (Matthew 28:18–20). This time they would go to the ends of the earth.

When Jesus had given these final instructions, he lifted his hands as their eternal high priest and blessed them. And right before their eyes, he was lifted up until a cloud took him out of their sight (Acts 1:9).

They stood there staring at the cloud. During the forty days since the resurrection, Jesus had appeared and disappeared. This was different. This was miraculous.

Suddenly, two men dressed in white appeared and said, "Men of Galilee, why do you stand here looking into the sky? This same Jesus, who has been taken from you into heaven, will come back in the same way you have seen him go into heaven" (Acts 1:10–11).

They hurried back to Jerusalem, changed men—men with a mission, full of joy, worshiping Jesus the Christ. Fearlessly, they went to the temple praising God (Luke 24:52–53).

God calls us to bear witness to the message of the gospel. Because Jesus died for our sins and rose again, we have hope. Does that motivate you to praise him and boldly carry out the mission he has given you?

Reflections

_____

_____

_____

_____

_____

Dig Deeper

1. The same man wrote the gospel of Luke and the book of Acts. Compare the ending of Luke's gospel in chapter 24:36–53 and Luke's continuation in Acts 1:1–11. What's the same, and what's different in his accounts of the ascension? How is Matthew's account different in chapter 28:16–20?

2. The warning Jesus gave his disciples (Acts 1:7–8) could be applied to the church in all ages: we have been told many things through prophecy, but we can't expect exact dates or details. Which of the warning signs in Matthew 24:33–50 apply to us?

3. The men in white (angels) told the disciples Jesus would return the same way he left. What else will happen on the event called "the Day of the Lord" in the Old Testament according to Zechariah 14:1–21, which is a prophecy of Christ's return?

Day 46
Our Blessed Hope

For the grace of God has appeared, bringing salvation for all people, training us to renounce ungodliness and worldly passions, and to live self-controlled, upright, and godly lives in the present age, waiting for our blessed hope, the appearing of the glory of our great God and Savior Jesus Christ. Titus 2:11–13 (ESV)

I spend so much of my life regretting the past. "If only I had or had not done_____" [fill in the blank]. When I'm not doing that, I worry about the future. "What's going to happen? What if_____?" [fill in the blank].

But God doesn't want us to regret or worry. God has promised that he will use whatever has happened or will happen for our eternal good (Romans 8:28).

Paul exhorted Titus to live in the present by waiting for "our blessed hope": the appearing in glory (future) of our God and Savior, who voluntarily died on the cross (past).

If we must look at the past, we should look at the cross, the first appearing of Jesus. In Titus 2:11–13, *appeared* and *appearing* are English versions of the Greek word *epiphaneia* "appearing or brightness." The Greeks often used *epiphaneia* to describe a glorious manifestation of the gods, an advent, a momentous arrival of the god's presence and power to help.[31] From this word we get Epiphany, the celebration of the coming of the Magi who sought the god whose birth was announced by a star.

When we look back at what Jesus accomplished for us when he died for our sins, our own past sins lose their power over us. His sacrifice removed the burden of our sins and erased the debt we owed. This is our hope: we have received forgiveness. David said, "As far as the east is from the west, so far has he removed our transgressions from us" (Psalm 103:12).

If we must look at what's going to happen tomorrow, we should look forward to the second appearing of Jesus. Paul defines our blessed hope as "the appearing of the glory of our great God and Savior Jesus Christ." Our hope does not lie in trying to forget about past suffering or in trying to prevent future suffering. Our hope lies in the glorious future appearing of Jesus Christ.

Is that the foundation of your hope?

Reflections

_____

_____

_____

_____

_____

Dig Deeper

1. Read Philippians 3:12-14, 20–21. What does Paul say about our citizenship in heaven and the hope that gives us? What will Jesus do to our "lowly bodies"?

2. According to Titus 2:12–14, how should we be living after we receive grace and salvation?

3. Read 1 Thessalonians 4:13–18. What was Paul's encouragement to the Thessalonians?

Day 47
When Jesus Comes in Glory

When [Judas] was gone, Jesus said, "Now the Son of Man is glorified, and God is glorified in him. If God is glorified in him, God will glorify the Son in himself, and will glorify him at once." John 13:31–32

Sometimes when we read Scripture, certain verses don't seem to fit. Sandwiched in between the revelation of Judas's betrayal (John 13:21–30) and the prediction of Peter's denial (John 13:36–38), Jesus spoke five times of being glorified.

If one of our companions had just gone to betray us, and another would soon deny he even knew us, we may have felt angry, rejected, offended—anything but glorified.

But Jesus looked beyond the present circumstances and saw that Judas's betrayal would lead to the crucifixion. God would be glorified as Jesus laid down his life voluntarily in obedience to the Father's will. Jesus's glorious resurrection would mean the redemption of many.

Jesus also looked beyond Peter's denial and saw that Peter would later boldly face the same religious authorities he feared when Jesus was arrested. Peter's spirit-empowered preaching on Pentecost motivated thousands to believe in Christ, and Peter's letters still speak to us today.

Jesus looked even further—to the end of time when he will again appear on the earth. Every eye will see him as he is glorified. *Glorify*, the English translation of the Greek word *doxazō,* is defined as "to praise, extol, magnify, celebrate, to honour, do honour to, hold in honour, to make glorious,

201

adorn with lustre, clothe with splendor, to impart glory to something, render it excellent."[32]

In Revelation 19:11–16, the apostle John described Jesus's glorious appearing: riding a white horse, wearing many crowns on his head, dressed in a robe dipped in blood as the armies of heaven followed him. On his robe and on his thigh, this name is written: King of Kings and Lord of Lords.

We who live between the times—between the first and second coming of Christ—need to look beyond our present circumstances toward the glory that lies ahead. Just as Jesus's birth, death, and resurrection fulfilled thousands of prophecies, be assured that his glorious second coming will fulfill thousands more.

Is hope springing up as you anticipate the glory that lies ahead?

Reflections

_____

_____

_____

_____

_____

Dig Deeper

1. Read Acts 1:9–11. How does the angel describe the first and second coming of Christ? See also Matthew 24:30 and Mark 13:26.

2. Read 1 Peter 1:13. What does Peter tell us to do to prepare for the revelation of Jesus? Does that refer only to the second coming, or could it also refer to Jesus being revealed in your life today? Why?

3. According to John 14:13–14 and John 16:12–15, how do Jesus and the Holy Spirit bring glory to God's name now? What is our part in bringing glory to God?

Day 48
Alive Forevermore

Jesus said, *"I am the First and the Last. I am he who lives and was dead, and behold, I am alive forevermore. Amen. And I have the keys of Hades and of Death."* Revelation 1:17–18 (NKJV)

In most artistic renditions, Jesus appears to be a gentle man. But that isn't the Jesus the apostle John saw in a vision on the isle of Patmos. The elderly, exiled apostle described the risen Christ this way: eyes like blazing fire, feet like bronze glowing in a furnace, a voice like the sound of rushing waters, a sharp double-edged sword emerging from his mouth, and his face shining like the sun (Revelation 1:14–16, paraphrased).

Intimidating, right? In fact, John "fell at his feet as though dead" when he saw his Savior and Lord (v. 17). What happened to the Jesus John had known on earth? Jesus had been glorified—clothed in his full splendor as the Second Person of the Godhead. John saw the King of Kings and Lord of Lords.

Many people attempt to pack the risen Christ in a box with their Easter baskets, much as they store baby Jesus with their Christmas decorations. But the risen Christ cannot be contained or dismissed. He sits at the right hand of God the Father with the power of a consuming fire and the authority of an indestructible sword.

In John's vision, Jesus identifies himself as the First and the Last—the self-sufficient, eternal I AM, who created the world, who appeared to Moses at the burning bush, and

205

who reigns in heaven. Jesus also says he's the Living One, that is, the sinless One who alone could fulfill God the Father's required payment for human sin, die on the cross, and arise from the dead. Because of this, Jesus holds the keys of death and Hades in his hands. He has earned the right to give all who believe in him eternal life and to sentence all who refuse his gift of salvation to eternal judgment.

The only proper response to the risen Christ—our king, judge, high priest, and savior—is to fall to our knees in worship before him as John did.

As we leave behind our Easter celebrations, let's hold on to Easter's life-transforming truth: King Jesus is alive forevermore, and through his resurrection power we can become the people he designed us to be. That truth is the bedrock of the hope that energizes us each day. Hallelujah!

Reflections

_____

_____

_____

_____

_____

Dig Deeper

1. In John 1:14, the apostle wrote, "we have seen his glory," referring to Jesus's transfiguration. Compare Matthew 17:1–8 and Revelation 1:12–18. What was the same about the two events? What was different?

2. What do Daniel 7:13–14 and Matthew 25:31 reveal about Jesus's return to earth? How do those passages complement John's vision in Revelation 1?

3. What is resurrection power, and what does it enable us to do? Consider these passages: Ephesians 1:15–23, Colossians 1:9–12, and 2 Peter 1:3–8.

Day 49
Here Comes the Bridegroom

Your throne, O God, will last for ever and ever; a scepter of justice will be the scepter of your kingdom. You love righteousness and hate wickedness; therefore God, your God, has set you above your companions by anointing you with the oil of joy. Psalm 45:6–7

What is the "noble theme" that "stirred the heart" of the poet in Psalm 45:1? Many scholars believe this psalmist was inspired by Solomon's marriage to an Egyptian princess. The writer of Hebrews makes it clear that this psalm is also messianic. Hebrews 1:8–9 connects Psalm 45:6–7 to Jesus's future reign: "To the Son, [God the Father] says, 'Your throne, O God, will last forever and ever.'"

Like Psalm 2, Psalm 45 paints a portrait of the Messiah that would have resonated with Jews who expected a conquering king—arrayed in splendor and victorious in battle (vv. 3–4). But it isn't a picture most first-century Jews associated with Jesus.

Jesus, however, identified himself as a king many times. For example, in Matthew 25:31, a few days before his crucifixion, he told his disciples: "When the Son of Man comes in his glory, and all the angels with him, then shall he sit upon the throne of his glory." And at his trial, he told Pilate, "My kingdom is not of this world" (John 18:36).

In Psalm 45, the psalmist praises the noble character of the king—a description that fits Jesus perfectly. Who else can truly be called "the most excellent of men" (v. 2)? Who else spoke with "lips … anointed with grace" (v. 2)? And although Jesus didn't wear a sword or clothe himself in robes of splendor (v. 3), he certainly championed "truth, humility, and justice" (v. 4). In miracle after miracle, including his resurrection, his right hand displayed "awesome deeds" (v. 4). All these characteristics, some veiled and others showcased on earth, will also characterize his future kingdom.

In verses 10–12, the psalmist speaks directly to the king's bride, advising her to leave her family willingly and to meet her bridegroom joyfully. The king is enthralled with her, and she should delight in his love.

When we apply these verses to Jesus and his future bride, the church, the message to us is clear: Our bridegroom is coming. Does that "noble theme" stir our hearts? Are we filled with hope as we await his appearing? When he arrives, will we greet him with joy?

Reflections

_____

_____

_____

_____

_____

Dig Deeper

1. Compare the description of the Messiah King in Psalm 45 with the account of Jesus's arrival in Jerusalem in Matthew 21:1–11. What similarities and differences do you see?

2. Read Matthew 25:1–13, another parable about a wedding. Compare Jesus's caution in verse 13 with John's declaration in Revelation 19:1–8. Are you ready for Jesus's return?

3. After Henry Barraclough heard a sermon on Psalm 45, he wrote "Out of the Ivory Palaces" (see next page). He drew many parallels between Jesus's first and second coming in this beloved hymn. What connections do you see?

"Out of the Ivory Palaces"
Henry Barraclough, 1915, public domain

My Lord has garments so wondrous fine,
And myrrh their texture fills;
Its fragrance reached to this heart of mine
With joy my being thrills.

Refrain:
Out of the ivory palaces,
Into a world of woe,
Only His great eternal love
Made my Savior go.

His life had also its sorrows sore,
For aloes had a part;
And when I think of the cross He bore,
My eyes with teardrops start.

His garments, too, were in cassia dipped,
With healing in a touch;
In paths of sin had my feet e'er slipped—
He's saved me from its clutch.

In garments glorious He will come,
To open wide the door;
And I shall enter my heav'nly home,
To dwell forevermore.

Day 50
Overflowing with Hope

May the God of hope fill you with all joy and peace as you trust in him, so that you may overflow with hope by the power of the Holy Spirit. Romans 15:13

Samuel Johnson, the English writer and critic once said, "He who expects much will often be disappointed." He was right, of course, from a human standpoint. We all journey through the valley of broken promises, misplaced trust, and shattered dreams.

Because people are fickle and life really does stink sometimes, we may make the mistake of transferring our human experience into the spiritual realm. We don't expect much from God because, after all, what if our expectations are too high?

The apostle Paul addressed that concern in his letter to the persecuted members of the church in Rome. He assured them that no matter how difficult their circumstances, they could "overflow with hope" because nothing could take God's joy and peace from them. Their eternal destiny was secure. God would not disappoint them.

Peter gave similar counsel to other first-century Christians scattered throughout the Roman Empire. He told them to praise God even though they were experiencing all kinds of trials because "the God and Father of our Lord Jesus Christ ... has given us new birth into a living hope through the resurrection of Jesus Christ from the dead and into an inheritance that can never perish, spoil, or fade—kept in

215

heaven for you, who through faith are shielded by God's power until the coming of the salvation that is ready to be revealed in the last time" (1 Peter 1:3–5).

Biblical hope isn't linked to circumstances; it's connected to the unchanging character of God and the certainty that his promises will be fulfilled. How do we know? First, we look back to what God has done—particularly the victory over sin and death accomplished through Jesus's death and resurrection. Second, we relish the blessings we experience each day: the power and presence of the Holy Spirit as well as the joy and peace available to us as we wait for God to complete his work in us. Third, we look forward to our eternal inheritance—life in heaven forever with our Lord and Savior, Jesus Christ.

On earth, yes, we will experience many disappointments. But as Paul told the Christians in Rome, nothing can thwart God's plans for us or separate us from his love (Romans 8:28–39). If we remain focused on those certainties, our hearts will "overflow with hope."

Is your hope rooted in those truths?

Reflections

_____

_____

_____

_____

_____

Dig Deeper

1. Read Romans 8:28–39. What does Paul say about God's character and purposes in this passage? Which of these truths encourages you most? Why?

2. Read Romans 15:4. What do you see as the connection between reading Scripture and hope?

3. Read Psalm 62. David wrote this psalm during a difficult time. What reasons does he give for putting his hope in God?

Endnotes

[1] "Spring," *The American Heritage Dictionary of the English Language* (Boston: Houghton Mifflin, 1981), 749.

[2] "Ashes," *Revell Bible Dictionary,* Dr. Lawrence O. Richards, gen. ed., (Grand Rapids: Fleming H. Revell, 1990), 100.

[3] This devotion first appeared in *The Secret Place*: *Devotions for Daily Worship*, (Valley Forge, PA: Judson Press), Spring 2009.

[4] The word used for *God* throughout Genesis 1 is *Elohiym*. In Hebrew, the final *iym* sound makes a noun plural. Therefore, the first sentence of the Bible indicates both the existence of a triune God—Father, Son, and Holy Spirit—and the Trinity's cooperative effort in the creation. (Note also the presence of the Spirit in verse 2 and the plural pronouns in verse 26.)

[5] "H4442 - *Malkiy-Tsedeq* - Strong's Hebrew Lexicon (KJV)." Blue Letter Bible. Accessed 22 Dec, 2018. https://www.blueletterbible.org//lang/lexicon/lexicon.cfm?Strongs=H4 442&t=KJV.

[6] Arthur W. Pink, *Gleanings in Genesis* (Chicago: Moody Bible Institute, 1922).

[7] "Hebrew Lexicon :: *Tsiyown* Zion H6726 (KJV)." Blue Letter Bible. Accessed 17 Feb 2015. http://www.blueletterbible.org/lang/lexicon/lexicon.cfm?Strongs=H672 6&t=KJV.

[8] "Greek Lexicon :: *Christos* G5547 (KJV)." Blue Letter Bible. Accessed 17 Feb 2015. http://www.blueletterbible.org/lang/lexicon/lexicon.cfm?Strongs=G554 7&t=KJV.

[9] "Rod" (also translated "staff"), *Revell Bible Dictionary*. Dr. Lawrence O. Richards, gen. ed., (Grand Rapids: Fleming H. Revell, 1990), 870.

[10] In addition to the passages mentioned in the devotion and the questions, see Matthew 26:64, Mark 14:62, Mark 16:19, Luke 22:69, Acts 5:31, Acts 7:55–56, Romans 8:34,1 Corinthians 15:25, Ephesians 1:20–21, Colossians 3:1, and 1 Peter 3:21–22. Numerous references also appear" in Hebrews: 1:3, 1:13, 5:6, 7:17–22, 8:1–2, and 12:2. See also "The Most Quoted Psalm in the New Testament, Part 1" in James Montgomery Boice, *Psalms, Volume 3* (Grand Rapids: Baker Books, 1998).

[11] "Outline of Biblical Usage" and "Strong's Definitions," "G5087 - *tithēmi* - Strong's Greek Lexicon (NIV)." Blue Letter Bible, Accessed 19 Jan, 2019. https://www.blueletterbible.org//lang/lexicon/lexicon.cfm?Strongs=G5087&t=NIV.

[12] The Pharisees had added "literally thousands of new commandments that were created to clarify the original 613 commandments" of the Mosaic Law. For example, to the Sabbath law, "39 separate categories of what 'work' meant were added that led to thousands of sub-rules," including how many steps a person could take and how many letters could be written. http://www.pursuegod.org/rules-pharisees/.

[13] Psalms 113–118 are known as the Egyptian *Hallel*, or the Hallelujah Psalms, sung in connection with the annual feasts. Psalm 118 was traditionally sung after the cup of wine served at the Passover meal (see Matthew 26:30). See *Oxford NIV Scofield Study Bible* (New York: Oxford University Press, 1984). Note at Psalm 113. See also *The Ryrie Study Bible* (Chicago: Moody Press, 1976). Note at Psalm 113.

[14] To see a diagram of Herod's Temple, including the altar on which the sacrifices were offered, go to http://www.bible-history.com/jewishtemple/JEWISH_TEMPLEHerods_Temple_Illustration.htm.

[15] Jesus didn't give this act a name, but the meal has come to be called *communion*. Paul called it "communion" in 1 Corinthians 10:16. Blue Letter Bible translates the word here as *koinōnia* meaning "fellowship, association, community, communion, and joint participation. Accessed 12 Dec 2018. https://www.blueletterbible.org/lang/Lexicon/Lexicon.cfm?strongs=G2842&t=KJV.

[16] "G4137 - *plēroō* Blue Letter Greek Lexicon (KJV)" :: Strong's Bible, https://www.blueletterbible.org/lang/Lexicon/Lexicon.cfm?strongs=G4137&t=KJV.

[17] "G1242 - *diathēkē* - Strong's Greek Lexicon (NIV)." Blue Letter Bible. Accessed 22 Dec, 2018. https://www.blueletterbible.org//lang/lexicon/lexicon.cfm?Strongs=G1242&t=NIV.

[18] For more information about covenant relationships and responsibilities, see "covenant" in *Revell Bible Dictionary*, Dr. Lawrence O. Richards, gen. ed., (Grand Rapids: Fleming H. Revell, 1990), 257.

[19] "Impute," *The American Heritage Dictionary of the English Language* (Boston: Houghton Mifflin, 1981), 662–63.
[20] "G3306 - *menō* - Strong's Greek Lexicon ((KJV)." Blue Letter Bible. Accessed 4 Mar, 2016.
[21] "Charles Studd," Wikipedia.com, Wikimedia Foundation, https://en.wikipedia.org/wiki/Charles_Studd.
[22] "G4851 - *sympherō* (KJV) :: Strong's Greek Lexicon." Blue Letter Bible. Accessed 17 Mar, 2016. http://www.blueletterbible.org/lang/lexicon/lexicon.cfm?Strongs=G4851&t=KJV.
[23] "G5087 – *tithēmi* Strong's Greek Lexicon (KJV)." Accessed 28 Dec, 2018. https://www.blueletterbible.org/lang/Lexicon/Lexicon.cfm?strongs=G5087&t=KJV.
[24] "G4418 (KJV)." Blue Letter Bible. Accessed 2 March 2015. http://www.blueletterbible.org/lang/lexicon/lexicon.cfm?Strongs=G4418&t=KJV.
[25] This devotion appears in a slightly different form in *Open Your Hymnal: Devotions That Harmonize Scripture with Song* (Raleigh, NC: Lighthouse Publishing of the Carolinas, 2010). Order a copy at http://tinyurl.com/ctfxtk0.
[26] "G3670 - *homologeō* - Strong's Greek Lexicon (NIV)." Blue Letter Bible. Accessed 28 Dec, 2018. https://www.blueletterbible.org//lang/lexicon/lexicon.cfm?Strongs=G3670&t=NIV.
[27] "Flabbergasted," Merriam-Webster Unabridged, http://unabridged.merriam-webster.com/unabridged/flabbergasted.
[28] Some scholars believe Salome is the wife of Zebedee, the mother of James and John and could have been Mary the mother of Jesus's sister (compare Matthew 27:56 and Mark 15:40 with John 19:25). To learn more about all the women of Galilee, consult a Bible reference book, such as *Unger's Bible Dictionary*.
[29] "G1021 - *bradys* - Strong's Greek Lexicon (NIV)." Blue Letter Bible. Accessed 28 Dec, 2018. https://www.blueletterbible.org//lang/lexicon/lexicon.cfm?Strongs=G1021&t=NIV.
[30] "G2962 - *kyrios* - Strong's Greek Lexicon (NIV)." Blue Letter Bible. Accessed 28 Dec, 2018. https://www.blueletterbible.org//lang/lexicon/lexicon.cfm?Strongs=G2962&t=NIV. "G2316 - *theos* - Strong's Greek Lexicon (NIV)." Blue

Letter Bible. Accessed 28 Dec, 2018.
https://www.blueletterbible.org//lang/lexicon/lexicon.cfm?Strongs=G2
316&t=NIV.

[31] "G2015 - *epiphaneia* - Strong's Greek Lexicon (NIV)." Blue Letter
Bible. Accessed 28 Dec, 2018.
https://www.blueletterbible.org//lang/lexicon/lexicon.cfm?Strongs=G2
015&t=NIV.

[32] "G1392 - *doxazō* - Strong's Greek Lexicon (NIV)." Blue Letter
Bible. Accessed 28 Dec, 2018.
https://www.blueletterbible.org//lang/lexicon/lexicon.cfm?Strongs=G1
392&t=NIV.

About the Authors

Nancy J. Baker is a writer, editor, and Bible teacher. She encourages biblical literacy using the Bible to interpret itself and making connections between the Old and New Testaments. At her church, Nancy co-leads women's Bible studies and has begun to present studies she has written, including *Seniors in Scripture*. She also leads a small group with her husband. They both have contributed to devotional booklets published by their church. Nancy creates quarterly biblical word search puzzles for *Power for Living*. She alternates with Denise Loock to write a new devotional Bible study weekly on digdeeperdevotions.com. For more info, visit digdeeperdevotions.com/about-Nancy/. She and her husband, Ken, live in New Jersey.

Denise K. Loock is an editor, writer, and speaker. Through DigDeeperDevotions.com, speaking engagements, and books, she shares with others the joy of studying God's Word. As a book editor, she uses her twenty-nine years of experience as an English teacher to help Lighthouse Publishing of the Carolinas produce high quality, engaging inspirational fiction and nonfiction books. She also accepts freelance editing projects. She is the author of two devotional books that highlight the Scriptural truths of classic hymns and gospel songs, *Open Your Hymnal* and *Open Your Hymnal Again*. For more info, visit digdeeperdevotions.com/about-denise/.

Contact her at denise@lightningeditingservices.com or info@digdeeperdevotions.com. She and her husband, Mace, live in North Carolina.

Dig Deeper Devotions is a website designed to encourage and enable you to dig deeper into God's Word on your own. Each devotion on the website takes an insightful look at a Scripture passage and provides a practical application. Then we suggest a few ways you can dig deeper into a word, a person, or a topic so you can develop the Bible study skills you need to grow as a Christian.

We don't publish a new devotion each day; we post a new featured devotion each week on Thursday or Friday. We encourage you to read the passages suggested in the Dig Deeper section and to use the study helps in your Bible to explore other Scriptures too. Hundreds of devotions are available on the website. Start exploring them today: digdeeperdevotions.com.

To Our Readers

If you've enjoyed this collection of devotions, please consider writing a customer review on Amazon. We'd also love to receive your feedback on this book. Contact us at info@digdeeperdevotions.com.

You may also be interested in our devotional collection for Advent, *Restore the Joy: Daily Devotions for December*, available on Amazon as an ebook and as a print book.

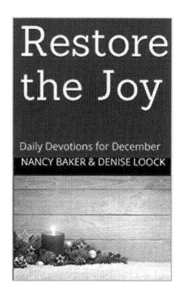

Made in the USA
Middletown, DE
02 February 2019